BEAMISH PARK HOTEL

30
years

First published in Great Britain in 2012 by Beamish Park Hotel.

ISBN 978-0-9572054-0-6

Photography by Clive Dickinson. Design and Artwork by Perro.
Printed and bound by Butler Tanner & Dennis.

Special Thanks to Paul & Julia Davison, Martin Black, Alan Russell, Clive Imber, Martin Charleton and Michael Powney.

BEAMISH PARK HOTEL

MODERN CLASSIC COOKING
A CELEBRATION OF 30 YEARS

This book is dedicated to the loving
memory of Stephen and Marie Walker.

PREFACE AND PERSONAL RECOLLECTION

It was with some surprise when Bill Walker, the owner of the Beamish Park Hotel, approached me and asked if I would be prepared to pen a few words to contribute to a book that marks the hotel's 30th Anniversary. As a regular guest of the family run hotel over the past 5 years, I accepted the request with great pleasure.

I have come to know and develop a close friendship with Bill Walker and his many loyal staff, who have made this my 'home from home' during the vast amount of time I have spent here.

Coming back as I have done, week after week, I have come to know and be known by practically everyone who works there. The reception staff have got so used to seeing me that they often book me in without being prompted as I pull up in my car.

I recall many evenings sitting at the bar with Bill and other mutual friends, where the conversations have ranged far and wide, but a recurring theme has been cars! It is these little things that are the difference between just using the hotel as a place to eat and sleep, and one which makes it a home from home.

This celebratory book is a selection of illustrated recipes that have been developed by Bill's son, Head Chef Chris Walker. The recipes are Chris's own fantastic creations and it is through him that the hotel has acquired an excellent reputation for its cuisine, a fact that is reflected by its many local regulars as well as those of its guests who, like me, come back time after time.

It is with Bill's gratitude for his many loyal customers that this book has been written.

I hope you enjoy this as much as I have enjoyed the hospitality of my friend Bill Walker and his many loyal and kindly staff who have looked after me so well over the years. Thank you all.

Quentin

May 1982.

Copyright 2012 Infoterra Ltd & Bluesky. Copyright 2012 Google.

HISTORY

The hotel opened on 18th May 1982, an auspicious month... the Falklands war had just started and 'This time we'll get it right (again)' by the England World Cup Squad was in the charts.

Originally, the hotel was three buildings; two bedroom blocks, and what looked like a large detached house at the front where the reception and restaurant were located. Unfortunately, as there was no conservatory walkway in those days, guests had to brave the elements to find their bedrooms, which was fine in the summer but not so good in the winter...

The bedrooms were also heated by wall mounted calor gas heaters which would definitely not be allowed by Health and Safety today!

The Tanfield Industrial Estate had just been built, Eveready Batteries was the largest company there, with smaller satellite companies in abundance and as the nearest hotels in those days were in Newcastle or Durham, the Beamish Park Hotel was the natural choice for accommodation... and the business was excellent!

ADDITIONS

The first bedroom extension in 1985 provided nine new rooms. In 1989, a further 22 rooms were added along with a spectacular new roof, which covered the courtyard area between reception and the bedrooms, a feature very much appreciated by guests in those cold winter months!

The lounge and bistro were both altered at the same time into their present form, although they have been refurbished regularly since.

The latest and largest refurbishment in 2010 included redecorating all of the bedrooms, new furniture, heating systems and bathrooms. The function suite, entrance and reception were also extended to create the welcoming, relaxing and contemporary rooms that our guests enjoy today.

THE GOLF ACADEMY

After many months of preparation and planning The Beamish Park Hotel Golf Academy opened its doors on 4th May 1998, a momentous day for the hotel.

We were delighted to commission Nigel Cabourn, an expert fashion designer, to design a very stylish sweater, with our logo on the arm, for the Academy.

The development includes a 20 bay floodlit driving range, a 9 hole, par 3 course and practice greens and bunkers.

The driving range is 'on par' with the best in the country, and offers the very latest in Golf practice facilities, with our Golf Pro Brian Ridley, a PGA Qualified 'Advanced' Professional, available to offer advice and tuition at all levels.

ACCOLADES

The hotel has collected a number of prestigious accolades over the years including an AA Red Rosette award for 20 years, a 2 AA Red Rosette Award for the past 16 years and BS5750 Quality Assurance.

We have also received numerous exceptional reviews in publications including Living North, The Evening Chronicle, The Journal, Business North East, Metro News, The North East Times and many more.

RECIPES

The Conservatory Bistro Restaurant has long been established as one of the finest places to dine in the area, having gained 20 consecutive annual AA Red Rosettes, including 2 AA Rosettes for the past 16 years; a fine testament to consistent high quality.

The main section of this book is devoted to recipes created by our Head Chef, Chris Walker.

Chris started work at the Beamish Park Hotel at the age of 16 and trained with our then Head Chef, Clive Imber, who was responsible for our first Rosette. Clive was an excellent Chef who nurtured Chris's interest in food and helped him to establish his culinary abilities.

Over the years Chris has developed his own personal style including 'revisiting classic dishes with imagination', to quote the AA restaurant Guide.

What you will find in the following pages are a selection of appealing modern and classic recipes with a twist, created by Chris.

Enjoy the book and happy cooking!!!

CONTENTS

SPRING VEGETABLE SOUP WITH BACON DUMPLINGS

Serves 4-6

For the soup

1ltr vegetable stock

1/2 an onion, peeled and finely chopped

1 clove of garlic, peeled and crushed

2 medium carrots, peeled and neatly chopped

1 celery stick, trimmed and neatly chopped

1 small leek, washed and neatly chopped

1 small handful of fine green beans, top and tailed, cut into 1cm pieces, blanched and refreshed

1 small cup full of broccoli florets, blanched and refreshed

1 small red pepper, deseeded and cut into finger nail sized dice

1 small tin of cannellini beans, rinsed and drained

Olive oil

For the bacon dumplings

8 rindless fat free back bacon rashers, roughly chopped

2 tbsps onion, finely chopped

1 clove of garlic, finely chopped

4 tbsps coriander, finely chopped

For the dumplings

Sweat the garlic and onions in olive oil until soft then leave to one side to cool. Mince the bacon in a food processor until very fine, then add the onion and garlic mix. Add the coriander, season and roll into walnut sized balls.

Method for the soup

Heat the olive oil in a pan, then add the onion and garlic and stir over medium heat for 2 minutes. Next add the carrots, stir and cook for 2 minutes, then add the celery, stir and cook for a further 2 minutes.

Add the stock and bring to the boil, then simmer for 5 minutes. Add the red pepper, leeks and dumplings and simmer for a further 5 minutes before adding broccoli, green beans and cannellini beans.

Serve in warm soup bowls.

ASPARAGUS, PEA & MINT SOUP

Serves 4

30g butter

1 small bunch of asparagus, tips removed and stalks chopped (asparagus tips can be used as a garnish or used for another dish)

1 white onion, finely chopped

300g fresh or frozen peas

1 x 500g packet of picked and washed spinach

1 small tin mushy peas

1ltr hot chicken stock

2 tbsps of chopped mint

Salt and ground white pepper

1 small tub of crème fraiche

Melt the butter in a thick bottom pan, then add the onion and asparagus stalks and sweat until they become tender but not coloured.

The next stage must happen very quickly so as not to destroy the colour of the soup.

Add the hot stock, reduce by a quarter, then add the can of mushy peas and bring to the boil. Then add the fresh or frozen peas and bring back to the boil.

Place in a blender, mix until smooth and velvety, then blend the spinach and mint.

Pass the soup through a fine sieve, season to taste and serve with crème fraiche.

CAULIFLOWER CHEESE SOUP

Serves 4

1 large onion, finely chopped

1 cauliflower, approximately 900g weight, peeled and roughly chopped

700ml vegetable stock

200ml double cream

100g mature cheddar, grated

1 tsp of English mustard

1 pinch of sea salt

Ground white pepper

1 knob of butter

In a large saucepan heat the butter, then add the onion and cook for approx 5 minutes, until soft.

Stirring often, add the cauliflower florets and stock. Gently simmer for about 35 minutes until all the ingredients are soft.

Blend in a food processor until you have a creamy thick soup. Then add the grated mature cheddar, English mustard, cream, seasoning and blend again until silky smooth.

Pass through a fine sieve, if the soup is a little thick add more hot stock.

Serve in a warm soup bowl, top with croutons and grated cheese.

PLUM TOMATO & BASIL SOUP

500g vine ripened plum tomatoes

2 cloves garlic, peeled and crushed

1 onion, peeled and roughly chopped

50mls olive oil

25g tomato purée

4 tbsps white wine vinegar

2 tbsps golden caster sugar

50g fresh basil, leaves and stalks

700ml vegetable or chicken stock

In a large pan gently heat the olive oil until warm. Then fry the onions, crushed garlic and basil stalks until they are soft and golden brown.

Meanwhile, pull the tomatoes off the vines and place them in the pan with the tomato purée, vinegar and sugar. Gently cook until the tomatoes are a soft pulp and the vinegar has reduced. Add the hot vegetable stock to the pan and bring back to the boil and gently simmer for 5 minutes, then remove from the heat.

In 2 batches carefully pour the soup from the pan into a liquidiser. Add the basil leaves, put the lid on, cover with a tea towel and liquidise to a smooth emulsified soup.

Finally pass the soup through a fine sieve, season and serve in a warm soup bowl.

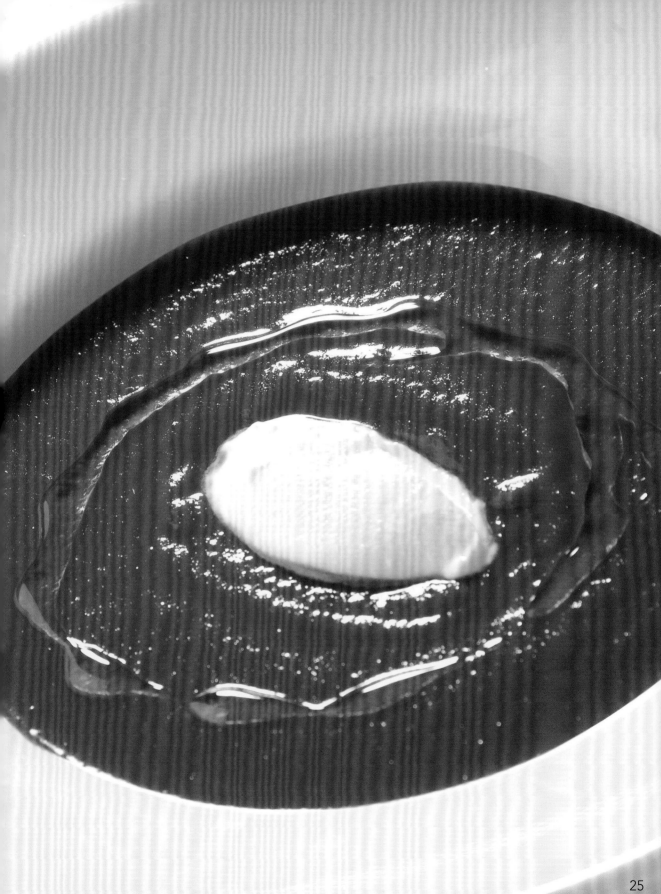

NORTHUMBRIAN HONEY, TOMATO & MINT SOUP

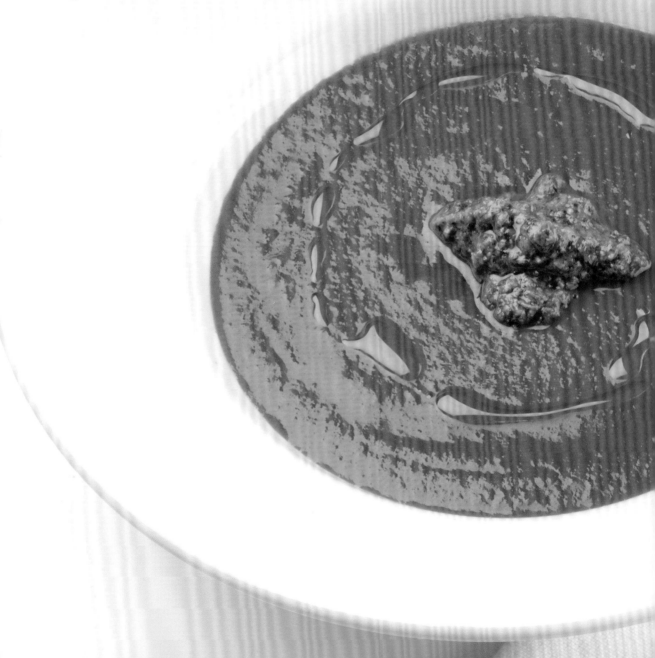

500g vine ripened plum tomatoes or 2 tins of san-marzano tomatoes

2 cloves garlic, peeled and crushed

1 onion, peeled and roughly chopped

50ml olive oil

25g tomato purée

4 tbsps white wine vinegar

2 tbsps Northumbrian honey

30g mint leaves

700ml vegetable or chicken stock

In a large pan gently heat the olive oil until warm. Fry the onions and crushed garlic until they are soft and golden brown.

Meanwhile, pull the tomatoes off the vines and place them in the pan with the tomato purée, vinegar and honey. Gently cook until the tomatoes are a soft pulp and the vinegar has reduced.

Add the hot vegetable stock to the pan and bring back to the boil, gently simmer for 5 minutes then remove from the heat.

In 2 batches carefully pour the soup from the pan into a liquidiser. Add the mint leaves, put the lid on, cover with a tea towel and liquidise to a smooth emulsified soup.

Finally pass the soup through a fine sieve, season and serve in a warm soup bowl.

CARROT & GOLDEN LENTIL SOUP

1kg large carrots, topped, tailed, peeled and grated

1 medium white onion, peeled and finely chopped

15g butter

170g yellow lentils, cooked until tender, cooled and drained

2 tsps mustard seeds

1ltr hot white chicken or vegetable stock

Salt and pepper

In a thick bottom pan, melt the butter, add the onion and sweat until tender with no colour. Add half of the grated carrot and cook until it doesn't have any colour. Add the hot stock and bring to the boil, then simmer for 10 minutes.

Place in a blender jug and blend until smooth. Pass through a fine sieve into a clean pan. Add the other half of the grated carrot and the mustard seeds and simmer until tender. Then pulse in the blender for 2 seconds until the carrot is roughly broken.

Return to the pan, season to taste. Add the lentils and bacon and heat through to serve.

PUMPKIN VELOUTE WITH HAZELNUT OIL

Serves 4-6

1kg French pumpkin, peeled, seeds removed and cut into 1cm cubes

80g unsalted butter

1 tbsp lemon juice

1ltr white chicken stock

130ml double cream

1 white onion, finely chopped

20ml hazelnut oil

Melt the butter in a thick bottom pan over a low heat. Add the pumpkin, onion and lemon juice. Stir before covering the pan with a lid.

Sweat the vegetables for 10 minutes, stirring every so often so that they don't brown.

When quite soft add the stock, increase the heat and bring the soup to a slow boil, then reduce the heat and simmer for 5 minutes.

Ladle the soup into a blender until half full, then purée for 2-3 minutes until very fine.

Do this until all of the soup has been blended, then pass through a fine sieve into a clean pan.

Season to taste, gently heat and serve drizzled with hazelnut oil.

If French pumpkin cannot be found, butternut squash is a good substitute. Hazelnut oil can be found in any good supermarket.

This pumpkin soup goes well with my black treacle bread (see page 210).

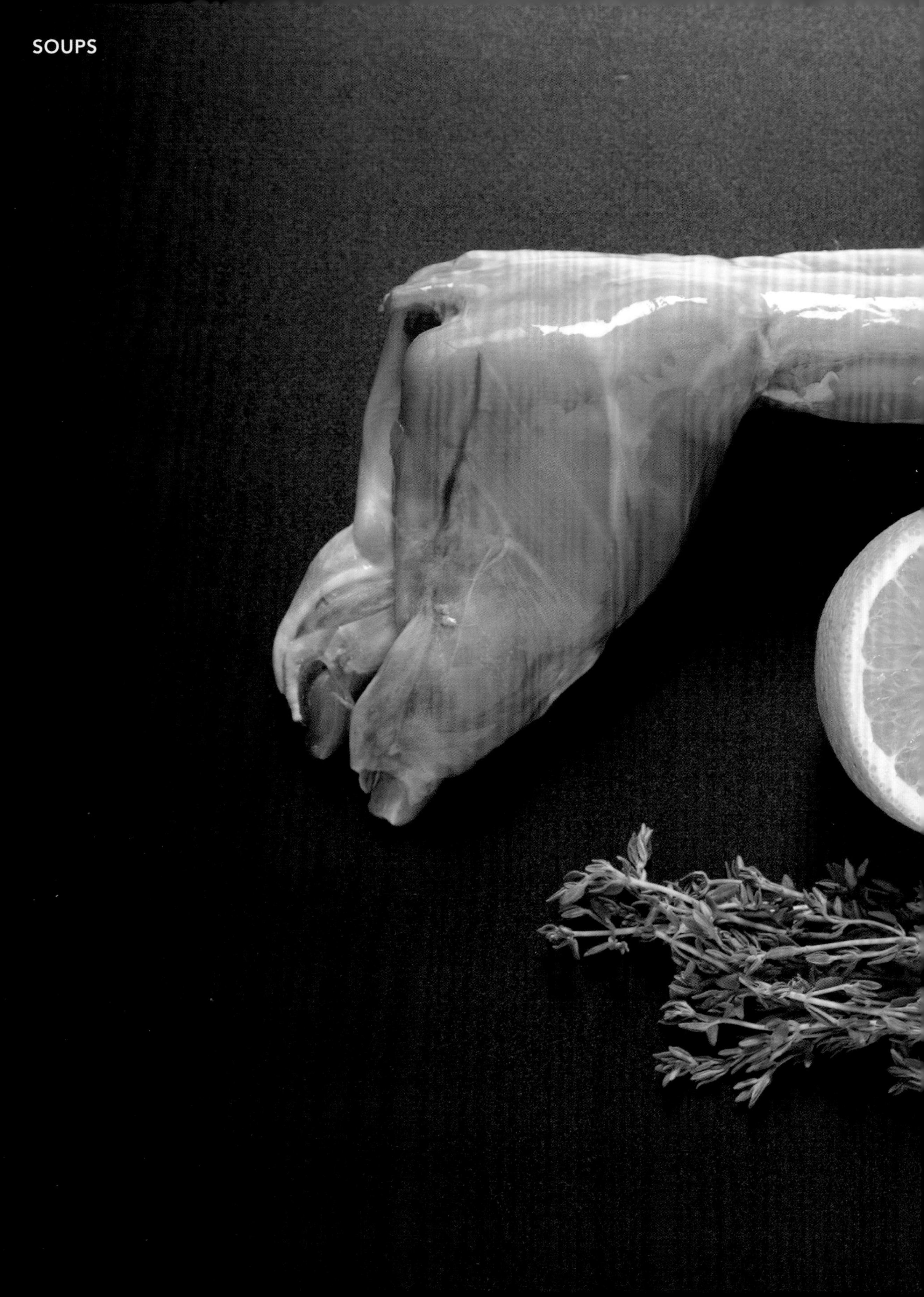

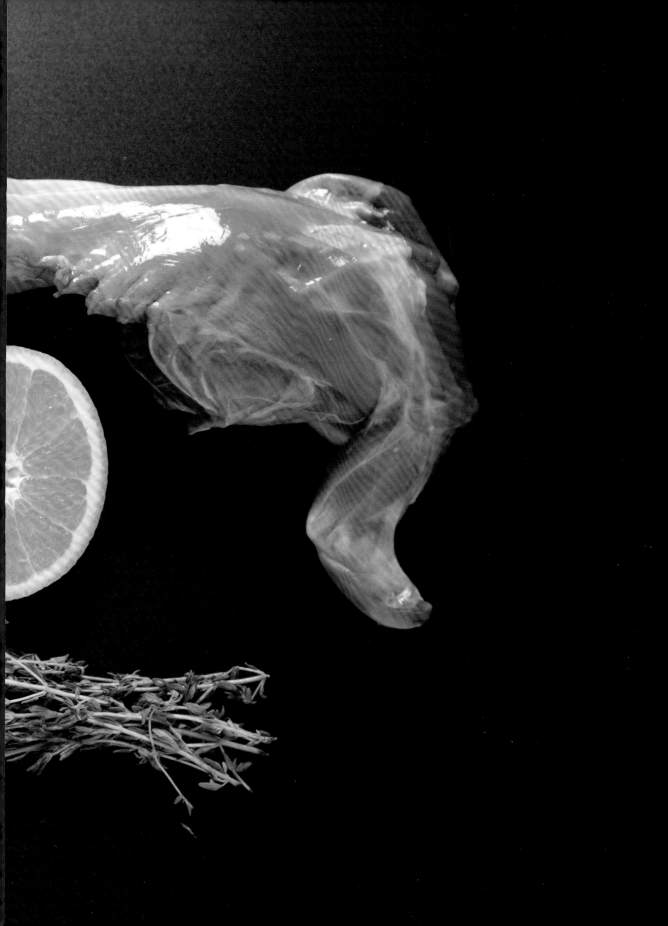

WILD RABBIT, VEGETABLE & RICE SOUP

Serves 6-8

1 small wild rabbit, gutted and skinned

3 carrots, peeled

4 sticks of celery, trimmed and halved

1 onion, chopped in half

2 cloves of garlic, peeled

6 black peppercorns

1 bay leaf

A few sprigs of lemon thyme

200g flat mushrooms

1 cup of long grain rice

Cornflour

50ml double cream

1 bunch of tarragon

1 bunch of flat leaf parsley

Put the rabbit into a large pot with the vegetables, bay leaf, thyme and peppercorns. Cover generously with water, place a sheet of greaseproof paper over the top of the pot, then a lid to make a good seal. Bring to the boil, then reduce the heat and simmer for 40-45 minutes until the rabbit is cooked through and tender.

Remove the rabbit, place on a tray and cover with a damp cloth to keep moist, set aside to cool.

Strain the rabbit stock into a clean pan, reserving the vegetables but discarding the garlic. Reduce the stock to 800ml, skimming as necessary.

Meanwhile, pick the meat from the rabbit and dice into 1cm size pieces. Cut the carrot length ways into quarters and dice. Do the same with the celery and onion.

Dice the flat mushrooms and fry in a pan with a small knob of butter. Cook the long grain rice and refresh under running cold water. Chop the bunch of flat leaf parsley.

Mix the rabbit, vegetables, mushrooms, rice and parsley in a pan. Thicken the stock with cornflour and mix the two together, bring to the boil. Finish with 50ml of double cream and seasoning.

STARTERS

ASPARAGUS WRAPPED IN SMOKED SALMON WITH BLACK PEPPER STRAWBERRIES

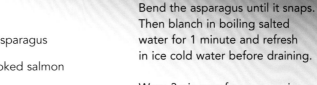

Serves 4

12 spears of asparagus

8 slices of smoked salmon

8 strawberries, quartered

Balsamic dressing (page 229)

Mixed salad leaves

Parmesan shavings

Cracked black pepper

Bend the asparagus until it snaps. Then blanch in boiling salted water for 1 minute and refresh in ice cold water before draining.

Wrap 3 pieces of asparagus in a slice of smoked salmon, continue until all of the asparagus is wrapped.

Once wrapped, place on a microwaveable plate and cover with cling film. Put to one side until needed.

Next, mix the strawberries with the cracked black pepper and set aside.

Make the balsamic dressing (page 229).

Microwave the asparagus for 1 minute whilst warming your plates.

Dress a few of the mixed salad leaves and place the warm salmon and asparagus on top. Then scatter the strawberries and parmesan and drizzle with the vinaigrette to serve.

BUFFALO MOZZARELLA, PEACH AND PARMA HAM SALAD WITH HAZELNUTS & BALSAMIC

Serves 4

16 Bocconcini mozzarella balls

12 ripe baby san-manzano tomatoes

12 blanched hazelnuts, roughly chopped

1 endive lettuce

1 radicchio lettuce

16 red basil cress sprigs

6 slices of Parma ham

50ml hazelnut oil

50ml balsamic syrup

Black pepper

2 ripe peaches

Sea salt

Olive oil

Pre heat oven to 120ºC.

Place the san-manzano tomatoes on an oven tray, drizzle with olive oil and a sprinkling of sea salt. Put the tomatoes in the warm oven for about 1 hour until softened.

Cut the peaches in half, removing the stone, then cut each half into three wedges.

From the heart of the endive lettuce, remove the paler crispy leaves and wash in ice cold water.

Remove the outer leaves from the radicchio lettuce. Using only the crisp leaves underneath, tear into pieces about 2 cms in size.

Place 3 peach wedges evenly spaced on a long plate. Cut a slice of Parma ham into 3 and crumple them slightly, before placing next to the peaches.

Top with the endive lettuce and radicchio, being careful not to over crowd the plate.

With a pepper mill lightly season the mozzarella balls and place 4 around the salad on the plate.

Then place 3 tomatoes around the mozzarella balls and add the crushed hazelnuts before topping with a few leaves of red basil.

Finish this off with a drizzle of hazelnut oil over the salad and a drizzle of balsamic to the side.

GOAT CHEESE PANNACOTTA
WITH CURED HAM, SUN BLUSHED
TOMATOES & MICRO HERBS

Serves 6

400ml double cream

100ml full fat milk

2 leaf gelatine, soaked in water

120g crumbled goat's cheese

Salt and white pepper

60g sun blushed tomatoes

12 slices cured parma ham, ripped

Balsamic dressing (page 229)

Small bunch of micro purple basil

In a saucepan gently heat the cream and milk. At boiling point remove from the heat and gently whisk in the crumbled goats cheese, then season.

Squeeze the soaked gelatine, before adding to the mix then leave to dissolve.

When cool, pass through a sieve and pour the mix into dariole dishes. Place in the fridge and leave to set for 6 hours.

Place each dariole dish in warm water to enable the Pannacotta to turn out of the mould smoothly.

Assemble in the middle of a plate, garnish with the ripped cured ham, sun blushed tomatoes, micro herbs and dress with balsamic dressing.

BEETROOT AND WASABI CURED SALMON WITH BLINIS & CRÈME FRAICHE

Salt mix

16 tsps rock salt

8 tsps sugar

4 cloves of garlic, crushed

2 sprigs of thyme

2 cloves

1/2 an orange, zested

1/2 a lemon, zested

1kg side salmon, pin boned, skin on

3 medium cooked beetroot, peeled and grated

1 measure of port

1 tube of wasabi paste

Lay the salmon fillet skin side down on a board and remove any little pin bones using a pair of tweezers. In a food processor combine all of the ingredients (except the wasabi paste and port) to make the cure mix.

Stretch two large sheets of cling film over a work surface, then lay the salmon skin side down on top. Gently prick the flesh all over using a cocktail stick and brush on the port before brushing on the wasabi paste.

Using a spoon, add the cure mix until the flesh is completely covered.

Completely cover the salmon with cling film, wrapping it tightly. Place on a large tray, then place another tray on top and press with a heavy weight.

Leave in the fridge to cure for 3 days.

Unwrap the salmon from the cling film and brush off the marinade and excess liquids.

Slice the salmon into thin slices. The cured salmon will keep in the fridge for up to a week and can be used just like smoked salmon.

Blini recipe

100ml milk, heated until tepid

15g fresh yeast

100g strong plain flour

1/2 tsp fine sea salt

1 free range egg yolk

2 free range egg whites

2 tsps sugar

2 tbsps beer

Begin by sifting the flour with the salt into a large bowl. Place the egg yolk in the middle making a well. In a pan gently warm the milk and beer until it is tepid then whisk in the fresh yeast. Remove from the heat.

Pour the yeast mixture into the flour mixture and whisk together until you have a smooth batter. Cover the bowl with a tea towel and leave to prove for 1 hour in a warm place.

Now whisk the egg whites and sugar until they form stiff peaks then fold into the batter.

To make the blini, keep the pan on a medium heat and add a small knob of butter. When melted add 1 tbsp of the batter mix.

After 40 seconds when the blini is light and puffy flip it over and cook for a further 30 seconds, before transferring to a wire cooling rack.

Repeat this process, adding a knob of butter to the pan each time. The batter should make about 10-12 blini.

TWICE BAKED WENSLEYDALE & CRANBERRY SOUFFLÉ WITH BUTTERED SPINACH & MUSTARD CREAM

Serves 6

200g Wensleydale cheese, crumbled

30g dried cranberries

30g butter

30g flour

250ml milk

2 egg yolks

4 egg whites

Salt and white pepper

150g buttered spinach

400ml mustard cream
(page 221)

Melt the butter in a saucepan and stir in the flour using a wooden spoon. Gradually add the hot milk and stir to prevent any lumps forming until you have a silky white sauce.

Then beat in the egg yolks and remove from the heat. Fold in the cheese and dried cranberries, season with salt and white pepper.

Whisk the egg whites until they form soft peaks then fold into the mix. Spoon the mixture into buttered deep dariole moulds.

Place the dariole moulds into a water filled bain marie and cook in a pre heated oven at 200ºC until doubled in size and golden brown.

Turn out and allow to cool at room temperature, then refrigerate until needed.

Pre heat your oven to 170ºC, place the soufflé on silicone paper and bake for 12 minutes until the core temperature reaches 63ºC.

Serve in a warm bowl with the buttered wilted spinach in the middle, pour over mustard cream sauce before serving.

BLUE SWIMMER CRAB 3 WAYS

Serves 6

Crab cakes

250g Maris Piper potatoes, peeled and halved

Sea salt and freshly ground black pepper

250g blue swimmer crab meat (back fin)

4 sprigs of coriander, finely chopped

1 fresh red chilli, deseeded and finely chopped

Juice of 1 lime and fine grated zest

1/2 tsp ginger, peeled and grated

Add the potatoes to a pan of cold salted water and gently bring to the boil.

Simmer for 15-20 minutes or until tender, then drain in a colander and leave to steam dry for a few minutes until dry.

Place in a bowl and mash until smooth.

Fold in the crab meat, chopped coriander, grated ginger, chilli, grated lime zest and juice, then season and leave to cool.

Divide the mix into 6 and shape into round balls (approx 80g each).

Place in the fridge and leave to firm up for 30 minutes.

To bread crumb your fish cakes

For the coating:

75g plain flour, well seasoned

1 egg, beaten

150g white bread crumbs

Place the flour, beaten egg and bread crumbs in 3 separate bowls.

Dip each fish cake in the flour, egg and finally the bread crumbs shaking off any excess.

Sit the fishcakes on a piece of grease proof paper and chill.

400g blue swimmer crab, white meat (back fin)

150g half fat crème fraiche

Salt and ground white pepper to season

25g snipped fresh chives

1 tsp freshly squeezed lemon juice

In a bowl place the crab meat, lemon juice, chives, crème fraiche and gently fold together using a spatula then season.

To make a quenelle you will need 2 spoons of the same size. With a spoon in each hand place the warm spoon into the mixture and drag the spoon towards you, scooping up a generous amount. Then holding the first spoon still, gently scoop the mixture out of the first spoon into the second. Continue to transfer the mixture from spoon to spoon using the same technique until you have a smooth, oval quenelle.

Crab spring rolls

400g blue swimmer crab meat (back fin)

1 small iceberg lettuce, shredded

Salt and black pepper

1 small thumb of ginger, finely chopped

1/2 bunch fresh coriander, finely chopped, stalks as well

4 sheets of spring roll pastry, each one 25cms square

1 egg, lightly beaten for glazing

1 baby gem lettuce, finely shredded

In a bowl mix the crab meat with the lettuce, ginger, coriander then season.

Separate out the spring roll pastry sheets and turn each square so that a corner points to you. Then brush each sheet with the beaten egg.

Place 80g of filling over each square. Roll the corner over the filling and continue rolling to the opposite corner. When you reach half way turn the edges in.

Press well to seal the parcels together. Roll the parcel around the filling and shape into a long thin cylinder.

Place on a plate in the fridge to chill and set.

To assemble the dish

Deep fry the crab cakes and spring rolls for 2 minutes or until golden. Quenelle your blue swimmer crab mix, slice your spring roll in half and line up all three along a warm plate.

Garnish with tomato jam and pickled cucumber.

OAK SMOKED CRASTER KIPPERS WITH PURPLE MAJESTY POTATOES & SWEET MUSTARD DRESSING

Serves 4

4 kipper fillets, skin on and deboned

1 knob of butter

100ml milk

1 small bunch of purple basil cress

1 carrot, peeled and cut into julienne

1 baby gem lettuce, washed and broken up

60g crème fraiche

1 quantity of sweet mustard dressing (page 233)

Potato Salad

400g Majesty Purple potatoes, washed

2 spring onions, finely sliced

Salt and pepper

Place the kipper fillets on a baking tray and cover with a bit of milk. Add a knob of butter and season.

Tray bake in a pre heated oven at 190ºC for 8 minutes or until just cooked. Remove from the oven and leave to cool slightly on the tray.

To make the potato salad

Place the new potatoes in a pan of slightly salted water and simmer for 15 minutes or until tender, then drain and leave to cool slightly. Slice to 1cm thick then add the spring onions and season. Finally add 4 tbsps of the sweet mustard dressing and fold together.

To Assemble

Remove the skin from the kippers and flake them. Place some warm potato salad in the base of the bowl, add the flaked kippers, julienne of carrot and basil cress. Finally pour over a little salad dressing and spoon over the crème fraiche to serve.

TEMPURA KING SCALLOPS WITH THAI CORNS, SUGAR SNAPS & BLACK BEAN

Serves 4

6 large king scallops

12 sugar snaps

8 Thai corns (baby corn)

Black Bean Dressing (page 229)

For The Tempura Batter

60g cornflour

110g plain flour

300ml soda water

Whisk the ingredients together to form a batter.

Blanch the sugar snaps and corn in boiling salted water for 2 minutes and refresh in ice cold water.

Slice each scallop in half horizontally.

Dip the scallops into the batter and deep fry at 180°C for 3 minutes. Then repeat the process for the sugar snaps and corns. Drain on kitchen paper and season with salt.

Warm your plates, place the scallops and vegetables and dress with your black bean dressing before serving.

LANGOUSTINES WITH WILD GARLIC RAVIOLIS

Serves 4

12 live langoustines

1 quantity of prawn and mascarpone cheese mousse

1 quantity of wild garlic pasta

20ml lemon oil

Wild garlic flowers

Parmesan shavings

Wild garlic pasta (makes 500g)

400g Tipo 00 flour

2 whole large free range eggs

5 egg yolks

40g wild garlic, blanched and chopped

Mix the flour, salt, whole eggs and egg yolks in a mixer until the pasta comes together.

Remove from the machine and knead for 3 minutes. If the dough is very stiff, you may need to put it back in the mixer with another egg yolk. Cut the dough ball in half and refrigerate for 20 minutes.

Dust the bench and pasta machine with semolina flour.

Using the pasta machine, put a ball through on the thickest setting ten times, folding the sheet into 3 each time to get a short, thick strap. Then turn it by a quarter and put it through the machine again. After ten such folds the pasta will feel sticky. Start to reduce the machine settings each time until you reach 0.5, the setting for ravioli.

To prepare the langoustines

Drop the langoustine in a pan of boiling salted water and cook for 2 minutes. Drain and refresh under cold running water. The langoustines will be undercooked but firm enough to peel. Pull off the heads and using a pair of scissors cut the underside of the langoustine and peel, taking care as they can be quite sharp. Refrigerate until needed.

To make the wild garlic raviolis

Roll out the dough as shown over the page, fill each section with a tsp of the prawn mousse and brush the edges with water. Then fold over the remaining pasta and cut using a crinkle cutter. Dust a large tray with semolina flour and carefully place the ravioli on it, making sure that they don't touch. Make 3 ravioli per portion.

Prawn and mascarpone cheese mousse

200g fresh water prawns, peeled and cooked

4 large tbsps mascarpone cheese

1/2 lemon zest

Seasoning

Place the prawns, cheese and lemon zest in a food processor and mix until puréed, then remove and season.

To assemble the dish

Bring a pan of salted water to the boil and drop in the raviolis. Lower the heat and simmer for 30 seconds or until the raviolis rise to the surface. Pan fry the langoustine in a little butter and season. Arrange on warm plates as shown and garnish with parmesan shavings, wild garlic flowers and lemon oil.

GARLIC SAUTÉED KING PRAWNS ON ITALIAN STYLE RISOTTO

Serves 4

12 large king prawns, peeled and deveined

50g garlic butter

8 parmesan shavings

4 slices pancetta bacon, grilled until crisp

1 onion, finely chopped

2 cloves of garlic, crushed

400g risotto rice

2 tbsps olive oil

1 knob of butter

250ml white wine

1ltr white chicken stock

100g freshly grated parmesan

8 sun blushed tomatoes

16 baby capers

Small bunch of spinach leaves

For the risotto

Bring the chicken stock to the boil.

In a separate pan heat the olive oil and butter, then add the onions and garlic and sauté on a low heat without colouring.

Next add the risotto rice and turn up the heat, and stir for 1 minute.

Add the white wine and keep stirring until all of the wine has absorbed.

Add one ladle of chicken stock and turn down the heat stirring continuously. Once absorbed add another ladle of stock, repeat this process until all of the stock is used. This usually takes about 15 minutes.

Taste the rice, carry on cooking until the rice is soft but still has a bite. Check for seasoning.

If you run out of stock before the rice has cooked, add some boiling water.

Remove from the heat and stir in the parmesan, sun blushed tomatoes, baby capers and spinach. Place the lid on the pan and allow to rest for 2 minutes. This allows the rice to fluff up.

For the king prawns

Heat a filament of olive oil in a large frying pan until reasonably hot.

Add the king prawns and sauté on both sides for about 3 minutes.

Then add garlic butter and season.

To plate the dish

Spoon the risotto along the plate.

Place 3 king prawns on top of the risotto and garnish with crispy pancetta slices and parmesan shavings.

HAND DIVED SCALLOPS
WITH BLACK PUDDING
& RARE BREED PORK,
SHAVED FENNEL &
APPLE PURÉE

Serves 8

1kg pork belly, deboned

250g black pudding

2 handfuls of flour

4 handfuls of fresh bread crumbs

2 eggs

100ml olive oil

16 king scallops, cleaned

For the apple purée

4 cooking apples, peeled, cored and finely chopped

100g caster sugar

2 tsps English mustard

Juice of half a lemon

2 tbsps water

For The Dressing

2 lemons

100ml olive oil

Mixed salad leaves to garnish

Pre heat the oven to 140ºC.

Place the belly of pork in a large roasting tray. Add water until it reaches a level that covers the bottom half of the pork. Cover with greaseproof paper, then cover the roasting tray with tin foil, making sure it is well sealed.

Transfer the pork to the oven for 4-5 hours and cook until tender and falling apart.

Remove the pork from the tray, discard the skin and reserve the fat in a bowl.

Pick the pork belly meat from the sinew.

Lay out 3 sheets of cling film on a work surface, then lay the pork in strips all in one direction close together.

Then spread with the fat, and place a layer of black pudding on top. Repeat the layering process until all of the pork and the black pudding have been used.

Wrap the cling film tightly around the pork and black pudding. Press in between 2 chopping boards using a 10kg weight, and refrigerate overnight.

Once pressed cut into 5cm x 2.5cm rectangles.

Pre heat the oven to 160ºC.

Coat the pork and black pudding with flour, then the beaten egg, then the breadcrumbs, making sure all sides are covered.

To make the apple purée, add the chopped apples, sugar, lemon juice and water to a heavy based saucepan and stir until puréed. Then purée in a blender before passing through a fine sieve. Add the English mustard and refrigerate until needed.

Finely slice the fennel and add the juice of 1 lemon and the chopped green leaves from the fennel.

To assemble the dish

Deep fry the pork belly and black pudding, pressing to colour slightly, then place in the oven for 5 minutes.

Heat a non stick frying pan until reasonably hot, add a splash of olive oil and seal the scallops for 30 seconds on each side.

Remove the pork and black pudding press from the oven and slice into 3, lengthways.

Place 3 fennel bundles around the plate and top with the scallops. Place the pork and black pudding next to the scallops and top with the apple purée. Garnish with dressed salad leaves.

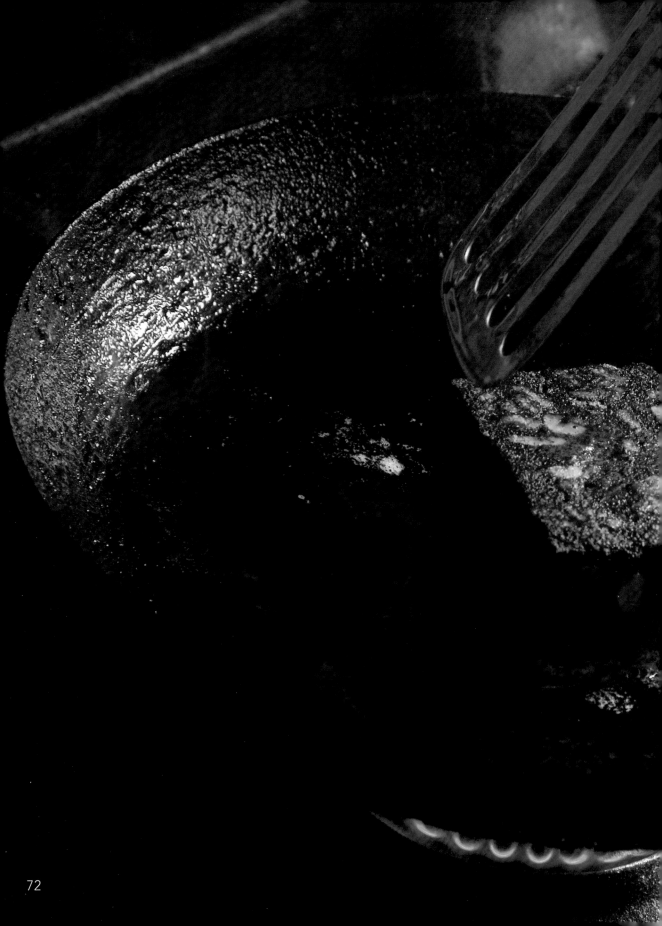

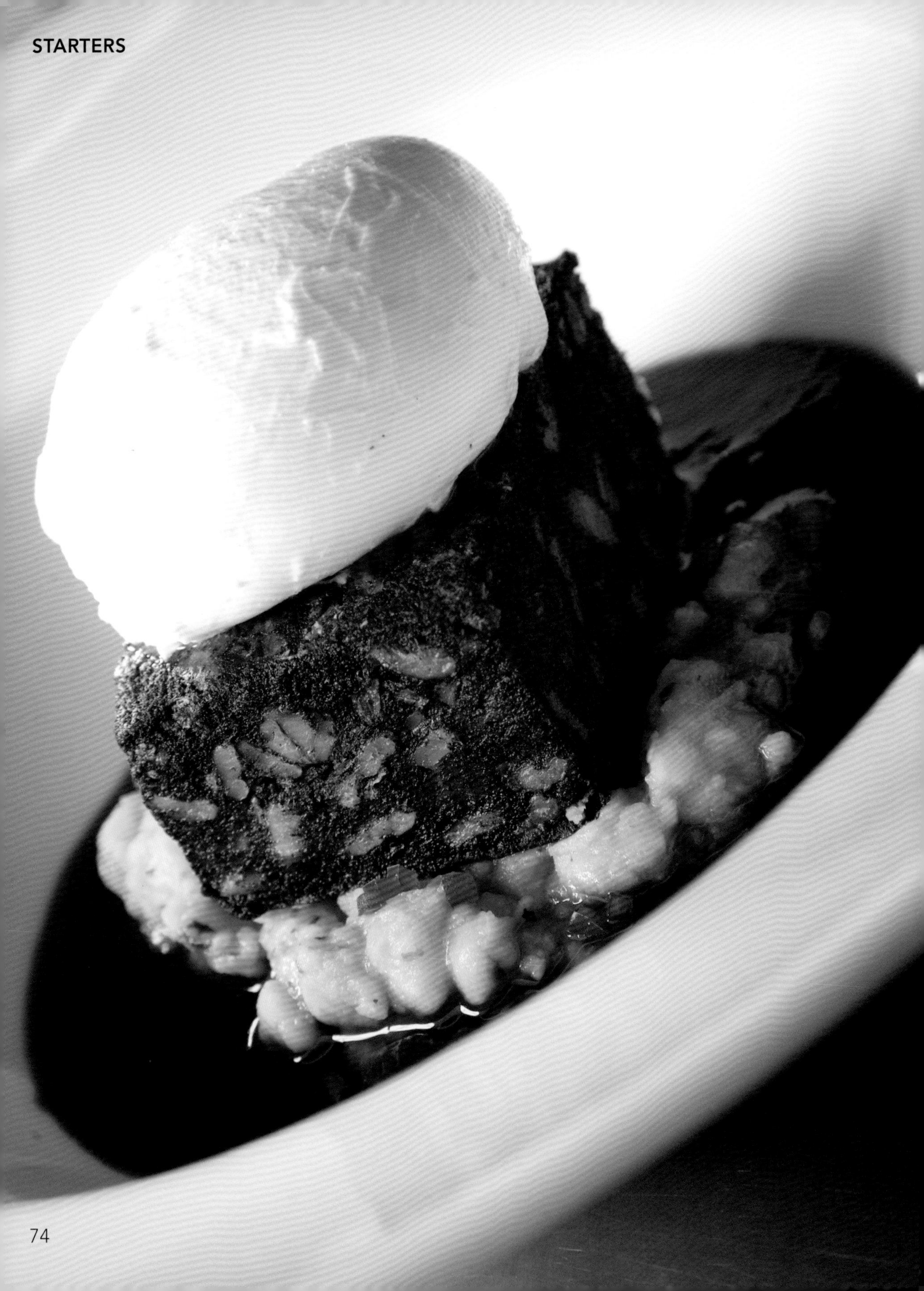

MARTI'S HOMEMADE BLACK PUDDING, SOFT POACHED EGG, MUSHY PEAS & DEVILLED GRAVY

Serves 8

1 onion, finely chopped

1 pint cider

200g smoked streaky bacon

3 sprigs of thyme

20g parsley, chopped

4 cups of black pudding mix

1 pint water

8 large eggs

Devilled gravy

300ml veal stock (page 220)

1 red chilli, finely diced

Mushy peas

500g frozen peas

50g butter

50ml water

For the mushy peas

Defrost the frozen peas and set aside 2 tbsps to add at the end.

Place the peas, butter and water in a small pan, cover with a lid and bring to the boil. Once all of the water has evaporated blend the mixture, then add the chopped mint and the rest of the peas. Keep the mixture warm until needed.

For the black pudding

(Black pudding mix can be bought from any good butcher).

Using a medium sized saucepan, soften the onion and picked thyme leaves in a little butter. When the onions are soft and a little coloured, add the cider and reduce on a medium heat until all the cider has evaporated.

Finely dice the smoked bacon and grill.

Using a medium sized saucepan bring the water to the boil, then add the black pudding mix and whisk until smooth. Add the onion and cider mix and chopped parsley then stir thoroughly.

Line a small terrine tin with cling film, fill with the black pudding mix and bake in a pre heated oven at 180ºC for 30 minutes. Remove from the oven and leave to cool before refrigerating. This allows the black pudding to firm up. We call this process 'setting up', it usually takes 4 hours, or overnight if you prefer.

Pre heat the oven to 190ºC. Then cut the black pudding into large 2.5 inch by 2.5 inch cubes. Pan fry, then place in the oven for 8 minutes.

For poaching the eggs

Bring a pan of water to the boil, add a splash of white wine vinegar and add the eggs, 4 at a time. Simmer for 1 minute, then plunge into ice cold water and repeat the process for the remaining eggs.

To assemble the dish

Bring a small pan of water to the boil, then spoon 2 tbsps of mushy peas into the middle of the serving bowls and place the black pudding on top. Warm through your veal stock, add the chopped chilli and pour the sauce over the black pudding. Then add the poached eggs to boiling water, heat through for 40 seconds and place on top of the black pudding to serve.

TANDOORI CHICKEN CROSTINI WITH LIME PICKLE POTATOES & CUCUMBER YOGHURT

Serves 4 as a starter

For the tandoori chicken

2 chicken breasts, cut into strips

2 tbsps tandoori powder or paste

1 tbsp natural yoghurt

1 small thumb of ginger, grated

2 cloves of garlic, crushed

1/2 lemon, juiced

Mix all of the above ingredients in a bowl and marinate for 1 hour.

For the lime pickle potatoes

1 small cauliflower, cut into florets

10 medium potatoes, sliced

2 tbsps lime pickle

1 bunch of coriander, chopped

In a small pan boil the potatoes and cauliflower florettes in salted water until tender, testing with a small knife. Drain through a sieve, transfer to a bowl and add the lime pickle, chopped coriander then season with salt and pepper. Keep warm and set aside until needed.

For the cucumber and mint yoghurt

150ml natural yoghurt

1 bunch of chopped mint

1 small piece of cucumber, finely diced

1/2 tsp mint sauce

1/2 tsp salt

Pinch of sugar

Mix the finely diced cucumber and salt, leave to stand for 1 hour, then wash under cold water and strain through a sieve.

Mix all of the remaining ingredients together.

For the pickled cucumber

1 cucumber, finely julienned

50ml white wine vinegar

2 tbsps sugar

Whisk the vinegar and sugar together until all of the sugar has dissolved, then pour over the cucumber.

For the crostini

1 bloomer loaf

Olive oil

Slice the bloomer length ways in to 1 cm thick slices, drizzle with olive oil, sprinkle with sea salt, then toast under the grill.

To assemble the dish

Place a frying pan on a high heat, add a little vegetable oil and fry the marinated chicken for about a minute on each side, or until it starts to colour and ever so slightly blacken.

Layer the lime pickle potatoes on the crostini, then add the chicken tandoori and top with the pickled cucumber.

Serve the cucumber and mint yoghurt on the side.

CHICKEN IN THE WOODS & LEMON CHICKEN TERRINE WITH BOUDIN NOIR

3 x 1.6kg whole free range chickens

3 lemons

1 small bunch of thyme

400g picked wild mushrooms (chicken in the wood)

300g boudin noir (French black pudding)

Seasoning

Preheat the oven to 200ºC.

Squeeze the juice from the lemons and rub all of this into the chickens, then season well with salt and black pepper.

Then place the squeezed lemons inside the chicken's cavity with the bunch of thyme.

Place the chickens in a deep roasting tray and cook in the oven for about 1 hour and 20 minutes, basting the chicken half way through using the juices from the tray.

When cooked remove and leave to cool.

Use a standard 30cm by 10cm loaf tin and line with cling film.

Pick the meat from the chickens and place in a bowl, dispose of the chicken carcasses.

Melt a knob of butter in a frying pan and quickly sauté the wild mushrooms until soft and golden brown.

Finally, squeeze a little lemon juice over the mushrooms and remove from the heat, then season.

To assemble the dish

Fill the lined terrine with layers of the pickled chicken meat then the wild mushrooms. Press each layer down.

Place the bourdin noir through the centre of the terrine then add more chicken and wild mushroom layers until completely filled.

Cover the top with cling film and secure. Press down and place a heavy chopping board on top. Then place in the fridge for 12 hours or overnight.

Remove from the fridge, lift off the chopping board then turn out the terrine on to an inverted chopping board.

Remove the cling film and slice into 1 cm thick slices to serve.

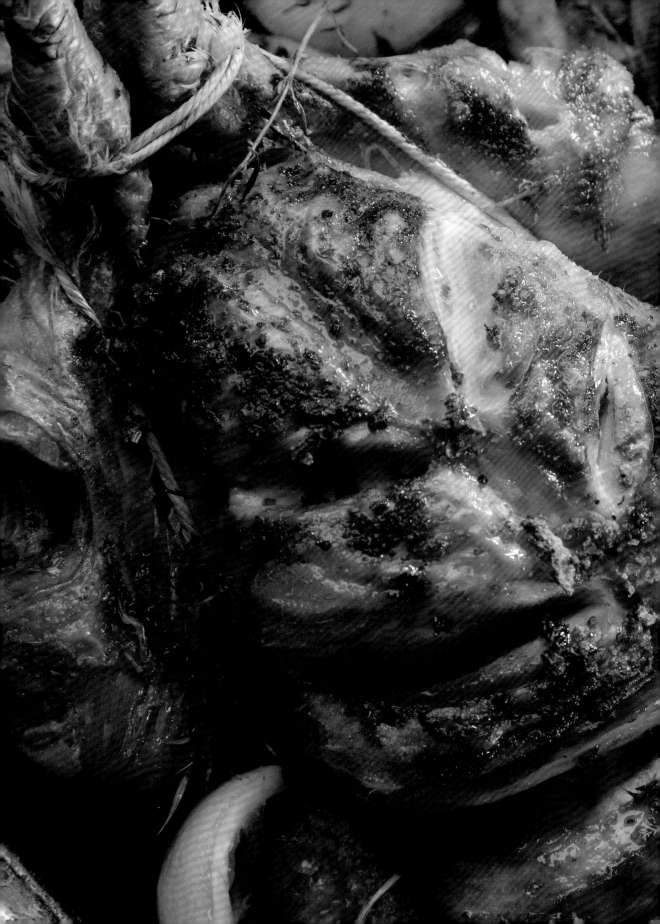

TEA-SMOKED CHICKEN WITH A CAESAR SALAD

Serves 4

2 chicken breasts

1 cup of rice

4 tea bags, opened, leaves removed, discard the bag

4 tbsps demerara sugar

8 slices of pancetta bacon

2 heads of baby gem lettuce

16 kalamata olives

12 parmesan shavings

4 buttered croutons

1 quantity of caesar dressing (page 229)

1 quantity of mustard dressing (page 233)

To smoke the chicken

Line a small deep 30cm by 25cm tray with tinfoil.

In a bowl mix the tea, sugar and rice then spread evenly over the tin foil. Place a wire rack on the tray with the chicken fillets on top. Cover the tray tightly with tin foil so that no smoke will escape. Place directly on to the hob on a high heat for 10 minutes.

The sugar and tea will caramelize and smoke, giving the chicken a lovely colour and smoky flavour.

Lift the chicken fillets off the wire rack and cook in the oven at 180°C for 5 minutes until they reach 63°C in the centre. Use a probe to determine the correct temperature. Remove from the oven, cool and refrigerate.

For the salad

Trim off the bottom of the gem lettuce, then break up the leaves and rinse under cold water.

Grill the pancetta bacon until crisp. Pit the olives and shave the parmesan using a peeler.

To plate up the salad

Place 3 baby gem lettuce leaves in the bottom of the bowl. Slice the chicken and layer it on the lettuce, building up the salad layer by layer adding the bacon, olives, parmesan and dollops of the caesar dressing.

Top with the buttered crouton and dress with 2 tbsps of mustard dressing to serve.

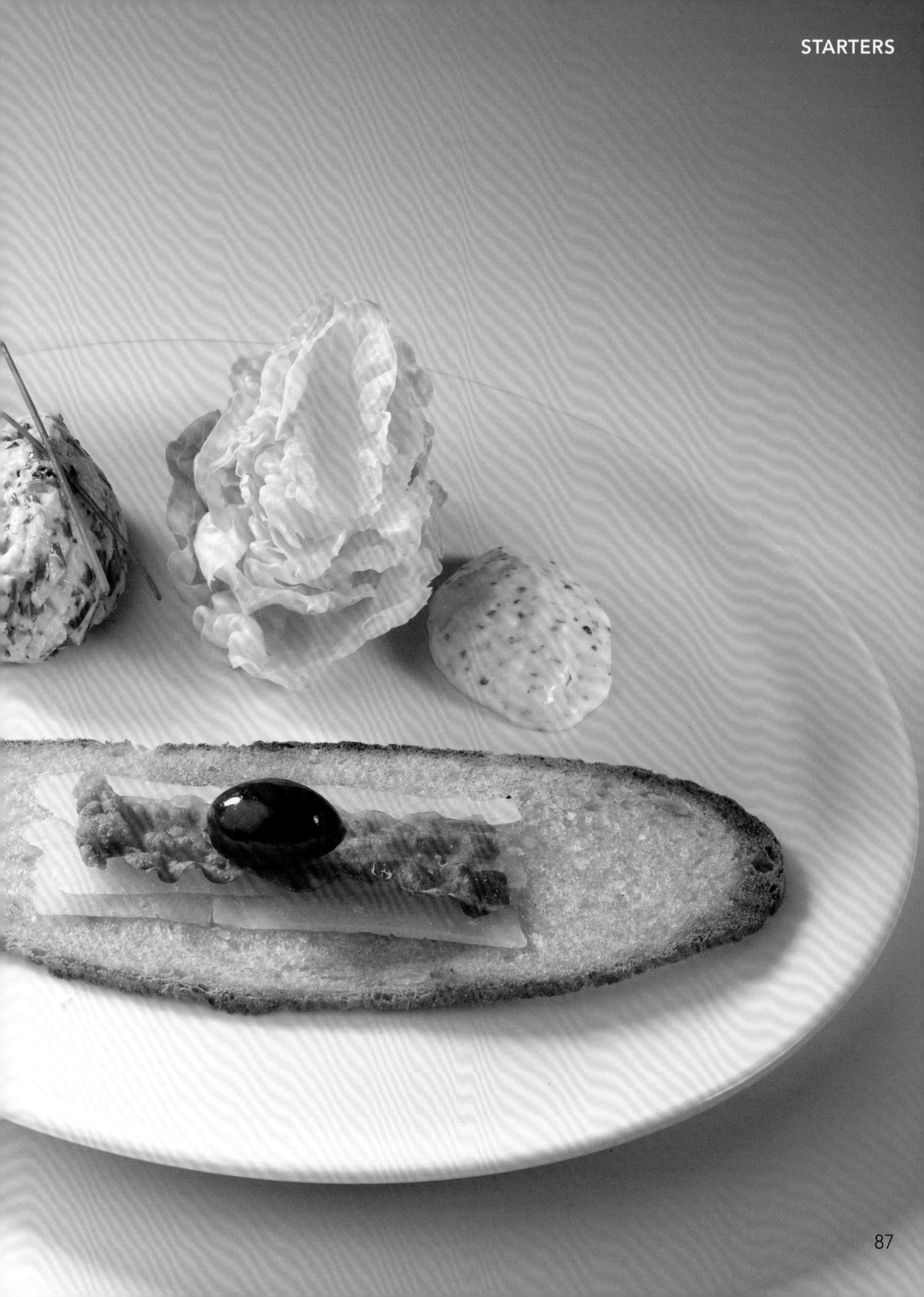

DUCK LIVER PARFAIT

500g duck liver

1 bay leaf

4 sprigs of thyme

30 slices of pancetta

350g butter, melted

350g eggs

3g maldon sea salt

milled black pepper

1 onion, peeled and finely diced

300ml port

300ml madeira

150ml brandy (cognac)

Lightly oil and cling film a terrine mould. Line with the sliced pancetta overlapping until the terrine is completely covered.

In a pan, heat the alcohol, onion, thyme and bay leaf, then reduce until almost completely dry.

In a blender place the duck livers, eggs, half of the onion mix and purée for 1 minute until smooth. Slowly blend in the melted butter until it is emulsified and shiny. Pass through a fine sieve and fold in the remaining onion mix and season.

Pour the parfait liver into the terrine and fold over the pancetta, then the cling film so that it is secure.

Place the terrine in a deep roasting tray and pour in enough boiling water to cover half of the outside of the terrine dish. Then place in a pre heated 150ºC oven and cook for approximately 45-60 minutes. The middle of the terrine needs to reach 63ºC, use a food probe to monitor this.

Remove the terrine from the oven carefully and remove from the roasting tray. Place the terrine in the fridge to cool and firm up for at least 6-8 hours.

To serve

Invert the terrine onto a chopping board, remove the cling film and slice into 1cm thick slices. Then serve with toasted brioche, chutney and salad leaves dressed with walnut vinaigrette.

SOY POACHED DUCK

1 whole Gressingham duck

2ltr water

300ml Shaoshing rice water

200g yellow rock sugar

3 star anise

1 cinnamon stick

1 x 10cm root ginger, peeled and sliced

3 garlic cloves, peeled

3 spring onions

300ml orange juice

3 red chillies, split

1ltr dark soy sauce

To make the liquor place all of the ingredients in a large pan and gently bring to the boil. Simmer for 30 minutes, then remove from the heat to cool, then pass through a fine sieve. Bring the liquid back to the boil in a large pan and place the whole duck into the hot liquid. Cover with a plate to weight it down.

Gently simmer for 2 hours or until tender. Remove from the heat, leave to cool, then refrigerate overnight infused in the cooking liquor so that the duck firms up.

Remove the duck from the liquor, strip the meat from the duck and discard the carcase.

The soy poached duck is nice in spring rolls with oriental table sauce or crisped up through the oven or fryer, served with salad leaves, a few nuts and asian dressing.

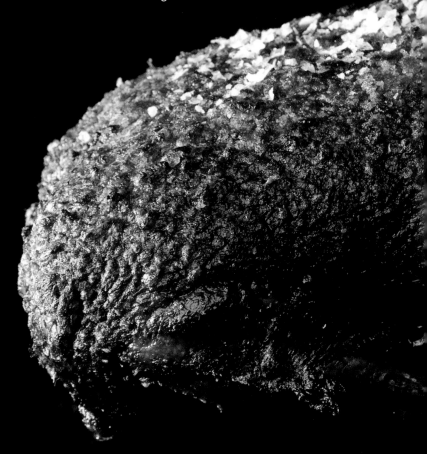

BROWN ALE RISOTTO
WITH BLUE CHEESE
& BACON

Serves 6

400g Arborio risotto rice

200g melton mowbray stilton, crumbled

300ml brown ale

6 slices of thick cut pancetta, cut into lardons

700ml white chicken stock

100g parmesan, finely grated

In a saucepan heat up the olive oil and squashed garlic, being careful not to brown the garlic. Then add the cooked Arborio rice and stir gently. Pour in the brown ale, stirring continuously until the liquid is absorbed. Next add 1 ladle of chicken stock, when this has absorbed repeat the process until you have a creamy textured and al dente risotto. Remove the garlic and fold in the grated parmesan and cooked pancetta lardons.

Divide equally between 6 warm starter plates and sprinkle with crumbled stilton, leaving this to melt into the hot risotto. Garnish each plate with crispy fried sage leaves and serve immediately.

POTTED SALTED BEEF WITH PICKLED
CUCUMBERS, POMMERY MUSTARD &
HANDMADE CRACKERS

Makes 4 pots

340g corned beef (page 141)

75g unsalted butter

100ml olive oil

1 bunch of spring onions, finely chopped

1 small handful of flat leaf parsley, finely chopped

Salt and pepper to taste

8 tbsps clarified butter

12 cornichons

4 tsps pommery mustard

Dice the corned beef into 1cm pieces and blend in a food processor with the soft butter. When the beef has puréed, drizzle with olive oil, remove from the blender and place in a bowl. Then add the spring onions, parsley and season.

Next spoon the beef into ramekins or pots. Smooth over the mixture with the back of a spoon, dipped in warm water and refrigerate for 10 minutes.

Remove from the fridge and add 2 tbsps of clarified butter to the top of the pots to seal them. Place back in the fridge.

The potted beef will keep for 10 days, as long as the butter has sealed the pots.

Handmade crackers

1 cup of flour

1/4 cup of polenta

1/4 tsp salt

3 tbsps sesame seeds

2 tbsps butter

1/2 cup of spring water

1 tbsp lemon luice

Stir 1 tbsp of lemon juice into the spring water. Mix all of the dry ingredients together then add the lemon water. Leave overnight at room temperature.

Pre heat the oven to 200ºC.

Make a well in the centre of the soaked mixture then add the butter and mix with a fork.

Place a ball of the mixture between 2 baking sheets and roll out until very thin. Sprinkle with sea salt and bake At 150ºC for 12 minutes.

Remove from the oven and cool on a wire rack.

Turn the oven off and place the biscuits back in to dry out for 12-20 minutes.

Remove the pots from the fridge 10 minutes before serving so that they reach room temperature.

Serve with 3 cornichons, 1 tsp of mustard and 3 handmade crackers.

MAIN COURSES

BUTTERNUT SQUASH CANNELLONI WITH GRILLED ASPARAGUS, TOMATOES & MASCARPONE

Serves 4

8 lasagne sheets

1 butternut squash, peeled, deseeded and diced

100g mascarpone cheese

60g bread crumbs

2 tbsps parmesan, grated

10 sun blushed tomatoes

1 egg, beaten

1 bunch of asparagus

Boil the butternut squash until tender then mash using a potato ricer and place the pulp into a cloth, then into a sieve to allow all of the water to drain from the squash. Refrigerate over night.

The next day all of the moisture will have drained away. In a bowl mix the butternut pulp, mascarpone cheese, egg, bread crumbs, grated parmesan, chopped basil and sun blushed tomatoes and season with salt and freshly ground black pepper.

If the mixture looks a bit wet, add a few more breadcrumbs. Place the mixture into a piping bag.

On a work surface, lay out a piece of cling film and rub with butter or olive oil and then place a lasagne sheet in the middle of the cling film.

Pipe a line of the butternut squash filling along the middle of the lasagne sheet. Roll up the pasta nice and tight, then wrap the cling film around the pasta, tie a knot in both ends. Repeat this process until you have 8 cannellonis.

Blanch the asparagus in boiling water for 1 minute, refresh and grill with a little olive oil and sea salt.

Microwave 2 cannelloni's at a time for 45 seconds until hot.

Cut one end of the cling film with a sharp knife. The cannelloni will slide out of the buttered cling film.

Top with the grilled asparagus, a few sun blushed tomatoes and parmesan shavings.

SAVOURY WILD MUSHROOM BREAD & BUTTER PUDDING

Serves 4

12 slices of 1 day old thick white sliced bread, crusts removed

500g mixed wild mushrooms

1 shallot, finely chopped

1 tbsp tarragon, finely chopped

1 tbsp flat leaf parsley, finely chopped

1 tbsp chives, finely chopped

2 large egg yolks

1/2 pint double cream

Salt and ground black pepper

30g melted butter

12 slices of chicken in the woods wild mushroom, thinly cut

Sauté the shallots and wild mushrooms in half of the melted butter until golden brown. Remove from the heat, drain and leave to cool. Then add half of the chopped herbs and season.

Grease 4 cappuccino cups with melted butter.

Mix the egg yolks, cream, herbs and salt and pepper well.

Use a spare cappuccino cup to cut 4 slices of white bread, these will form the lids. Then use a medium sized pastry cutter to cut 4 discs to form the bases. Cut the remaining slices of bread in half length ways to form the sides of the puddings.

To assemble, dip the medium cut bread discs in herby egg mix and place in the bottom of the greased cups, then do the same with the long cut bread slices and line the sides of the cup.

Fill the 4 cups with the wild mushroom mix, packing tightly and filling each cup. Dip each top layer bread disc in the herby egg mix and place on top.

Press down well with your hands to seal them, this will produce a lot of egg liquid, which can be wiped away with a damp cloth. Seal the cups with cling film and microwave for 45 seconds then turn out into a bowl or plate.

Next pan fry the chicken in the woods wild mushroom in a little butter for 30 seconds, and add a squeeze of lemon juice and seasoning. Place the mushroom around the pudding and serve with mustard cream.

This is a very good vegetarian dish, it can also be made in smaller cups to accompany meat dishes.

LINE CAUGHT HALIBUT, WILD GARLIC MASH, WHITE BEANS, TOMATO & CHORIZO

Serves 4

4 x 140g chunky line caught halibut portions

1 quantity of yukon gold mash potato

1 bunch of wild garlic, picked, washed, blanched and puréed

For the white bean, tomato and chorizo

1/2 tin of cannellini beans, or any white bean

1 tomato, cut into 0.5cm dice

1 small chorizo sausage, finely sliced

1 small onion, finely sliced

1 tbsp tomato ketchup

1 tbsp coriander, chopped

8 sun blushed tomatoes, chopped

Splash of worcester sauce

50ml olive oil

Sauté the chorizo in olive oil until crispy but not burnt then add the onion and tomato and continue to cook until softened.

Add the ketchup, worcester sauce, beans and coriander. If you find the sauce a little thick, add a splash of water.

Check the seasoning and keep warm until needed.

Add the wild garlic purée to the mash and keep warm.

Pre heat the oven to 180ºC and season the halibut fillets.

Heat a filament of butter substitute (whirl) in a frying pan and add the fish, skin side down. Fry for 1 minute, turn over, and fry for a further minute. Add a knob of butter and fry for 30 seconds more, taking care not to burn the butter.

Remove from the pan, place on a non stick baking tray and cook in the oven for 6 minutes. Times will vary depending on the thickness of the fish fillets.

Warm the plates in an oven or under a grill then spoon your mash onto the side. Add the white bean, tomato and chorizo sauce then place your fish fillets alongside. Garnish with wild garlic flowers.

BEER BATTERED FISH & CHIPS

Serves 4

4 x 140g chunky cod portions

1kg Maris Piper potatoes

For the batter

200g flour

200g cornflour

500ml beer

1/4 tsp baking powder

1 pinch of cayenne pepper

1 pinch of salt

1 tbsp soy sauce

1 egg yolk

Mix all of the dry ingredients together and whisk in the beer, soy sauce and egg yolk until smooth. Refrigerate until needed.

Peel the potatoes and cut length ways into chips and blanch in the deep fat fryer at 250ºC until soft.

Drain and store on a tray until needed, turn the fryer up to 350ºC and dip the batter coated cod fillet into the fryer.

The cod will take 5-7 minutes to cook, depending on the thickness. When the batter is golden, drain from the fryer using a slotted spoon.

Then add the chips and fry until crisp and golden. Remove from the fryer and drain on a paper towel. Season with salt and serve with tartar sauce and lemon.

DOVER SOLE WITH BROWN SHRIMPS, GRAPES, CUCUMBER & CHAMPAGNE BUTTER SAUCE

Serves 4

4 dover sole, skinned, gutted, with head removed

100g brown shrimps

1 cucumber, balled using a Parisienne scoupe

1 bunch of grapes

175ml champagne

1 bunch of dill, chopped

3 shallots, finely diced

250g unsalted butter

Add a knob of butter to a small saucepan then add the shallots and soften slightly on a low heat being careful not to brown.

When soft, add the champagne and reduce until totally evaporated.

Next dice the butter into 1cm cubes and add the shallots. Whisking constantly add the cubes of butter, 1 piece at a time until completely melted. If the sauce starts to split, add 1 tbsp of hot water.

Set aside until needed.

Pre heat the oven to 180°C, lightly oil a baking tray and place the sole in the middle of the tray.

Rub the fish with clarified butter, season with salt and pepper and bake in the oven for 10 minutes.

Once the sole is ready you will be able to easily remove the bone.

To do this, using a fish slice, pull away the fins from the top to the bottom of the sole, then run the slice straight down the middle of the fish. Now you will be able to feel the bone, separate the 2 fillets and remove.

Stack 2 fillets on top of another 2 and keep warm.

Blanch the cucumber in salted water for 30 seconds, drain and mix in a small pan with the grapes, shrimps and dill, then add the butter sauce.

Warm through, season with salt and pepper to taste.

Pour over the fish and serve with a wedge of lemon.

THAI BAKED SEA BASS WITH COCONUT JASMINE RICE & MANGO SALSA

Serves 4 as a main course

4 line caught sea bass, filleted

4 tbsps thai curry paste

2 cups of jasmine rice

1/4 of a block of coconut cream

1 ripe mango, diced

1 red chilli, finely diced

1 lime, juiced

1 handful of coriander, chopped

1/4 red onion, finely diced

To garnish

Coriander

Sesame oil

Sesame seeds

Black sesame seeds

Thai curry paste

1 bunch of coriander

1 thumb of ginger, grated

2 cloves of garlic, crushed

4 lime leaves, finely chopped

1 bunch of spring onions

2 green chillis, roughly chopped

1 stick lemon grass, finely chopped

25ml sesame oil

25ml vegetable oil

splash of thai fish sauce

For the thai curry paste

Blend all of the ingredients in a food processor until chopped to a paste.

For the sea bass

Lay a 30cm long piece of cling film on the work surface and add 1 fillet of sea bass.

Then spread 1 tbsp of thai curry paste over the fish fillet covering the edges. Place the other fillet on top and roll both fillets together tightly in the cling film, folding in both edges.

Bake in the oven for 15 minutes at 190ºC. This technique allows the fish to steam in its own juices and keeps the sea bass extremely moist.

Whilst your fish is cooking prepare the coconut rice and mango salsa.

For the coconut rice

Boil the rice for 10 minutes in salted water until tender. Once cooked drain through a sieve and season with salt, add the grated coconut and set aside until required.

For the mango salsa

Mix the diced mango, red chilli, diced red onion coriander and lime juice together and lightly season.

To assemble the dish

Place the coconut rice in the middle of your plate, then cut the sea-bass out of the cling film and place on top of the rice. Spoon over the mango salsa and dress the coriander with the sesame oil and seeds, place on top of the fish and serve.

This dish is quite easy to prepare for a dinner party because all the elements of the dish are prepared in advance and all you need to do is cook the sea bass at the last minute.

GRILLED MIXED FISH & SHELLFISH WITH LEMON POTATOES & FIRE ROAST SWEET PEPPERS

Serves 4

2 sea bass fillets, halved

4 x 50g pieces of salmon

4 x 50g pieces of tuna

4 king prawns, cleaned

4 king scallops, cleaned

4 sweet red peppers

16 turned lemon potatoes

Juice of 2 lemons

10g coriander or basil, chopped

2 semi-dried plum tomatoes, halved

10ml olive oil

For the lemon potatoes

1 lemon, cut into wedges

8 sprigs of fresh thyme

1 tsp sea salt

500g charlotte potatoes

4 tbsps olive oil

4 tbsps lemon juice

Peel and trim the charlotte potatoes into barrel shapes and place them in a heavy bottom pan with the lemon, sea salt and thyme. Cover with water and bring to the boil. Gently simmer for 15 minutes or until tender, then drain and

place in a bowl and season. Pour on the olive oil and lemon juice, keep warm and leave to infuse.

Fire roast sweet red peppers

4 whole red peppers

4 bamboo wooden skewers, soaked in hot water

1 freezer bag

Push the skewers completely through each pepper. Turn the stove to a medium high heat with a fairly large flame. Place the peppers on the burners making sure they are close to the flames. Leave the peppers over the flames rotating them on the skewers every 4-5 minutes.

Once the skin has turned black and crispy, remove from the heat. Place them in a plastic freezer bag and close. The steam will help when removing the skin from the peppers.

When cool, rub the peppers between your fingers and hands, once all the skin is removed, place the peppers on a chopping board, cut the tops off each pepper and slice down one side exposing the inner seed cavity. Scrape off the white membrane and inner seeds then discard them.

Cut into thin slices and add a pinch of sea salt, the juice of 2 lemons and 4 tbsps of olive oil, keep warm until needed.

Cooking the fish

In a large non stick frying pan heat the olive oil, add the king prawns, fry on each side for 2 minutes until golden brown and cooked.

Next, add the salmon with the tuna, then the sea bass and cook only for 1 minute, then turn over until golden brown. Finally add the king scallops and fry for 1 minute until golden brown then turn over. Repeat this until all of the shellfish is golden brown. Finally, squeeze over the lemon juice.

To assemble

Using 4 large bowls, place 4 hot new potatoes in the base of each, then gently stack a piece of shellfish on top of this.

Finally place some of the warm roast red pepper slices onto the top of the dish. Drizzle over the excess juice from the peppers and serve.

119

BLACKENED SALMON, FRESH CRAB CAKES & CITRUS YOGHURT & SALTED CUCUMBERS

For the crab cakes

Makes 8 cakes

400g crab meat

500g baking potatoes, peeled and grated

250g sweet potatoes, peeled and grated

30g cornflour

40ml lemon juice

1 small egg, beaten

1/2 cup of spring onions, finely sliced

1/2 cup of coriander leaves, chopped

50ml olive oil

Salt and pepper

Squeeze as much liquid from the grated potatoes as possible then discard. Mix in the egg, cornflour, salt, pepper and spring onions.

Divide into 8 cakes, 8cm round by 1cm thick. Heat a non stick rosti pan, brush with a little olive oil, fry the cakes on each side until golden and place on a tray ready to go in the oven.

Mix the crab meat, lemon juice, olive oil and season.

Blackened spice mix

2 tbsps paprika

2 tbsps dried thyme

2 tbsps dried oregano

1 tbsp garlic powder

1 tbsp demerrera sugar

1 tbsp onion powder

1 tbsp ground cumin

1 tbsp cayenne pepper or chilli flakes

2 tbsps salt

Mix all of the ingredients together and store in an air tight container.

Citrus yoghurt

This recipe makes 500ml, when stored in an air tight jar it will keep for over a week. It also goes well with spicy chicken.

300ml thick natural yoghurt

50ml olive oil

1 lemon

1 lime

1 orange

1 tbsp sugar

Line a sieve with a piece of muslin cloth and pour in the yoghurt. Fold over the cloth and place the sieve over a container and refrigerate overnight.

Remove from the fridge and tip the yoghurt into a bowl, discard the liquid.

Mix the yoghurt, olive oil and sugar together, then add the juice of the orange and lime and the zest of lemon. Next add a pinch of salt and taste, add a little more sugar if needed.

Serves 4

4 x 160g organic salmon portions, pin boned, skinned

8 fresh crab cakes

1 cucumber, julienned

10g sea salt

1 quantity of blackened spice

2 tbsps vegetable oil

Mix the cucumber and salt together, place in a sieve and leave to drain for 30 minutes.

Pre heat the oven to 180ºC.

Dust the salmon fillets with the blackening spice and leave to sit for 5 minutes.

Heat your frying pan until very hot, add the vegetable oil and cook the salmon for 90 seconds without moving it. Turn over the salmon and cook for another 90 seconds, then remove. Cook in the oven for 3 minutes, then leave in a warm place for 5 minutes.

Whilst the salmon is resting warm the potato cakes in the oven for 2 minutes.

Place a crab cake on each plate then add a fourth of the crab meat, before placing another cake on top.

Then position the cucumber on top, drizzle with olive oil and place the salmon next to that. Serve with the citrus yoghurt and a crisp salad.

POACHED SPRING SALMON WITH SPRING VEGETABLES, CHARLOTTE POTATOES & HERB OLIVE OIL EMULSION

Serves 4

4 x 140g organic spring salmon fillets

8 asparagus spears

4 flowering baby courgettes

4 spring onions

2 cups of fresh herbs

1 cup of broad beans, blanched and podded

16 charlotte potatoes, turned and blanched

4 tbsps herb emulsion

1 quantity of court bouillon (see page 215)

Herb Emulsion

3 slices of day old bread, crusts removed

3 tbsps red wine vinegar

1/3 cup of tarragon leaves

1 clove of garlic, minced

60ml olive oil

Salt and pepper

To make the emulsion

Moisten the bread with the red wine vinegar until completely absorbed. Place the bread, tarragon and garlic in a food processor and turn it on, pouring the olive oil in slowly until it's well blended. Then season to taste and store in a sealed jar in the fridge until needed.

To cook the salmon and vegetables

Bring the court bouillon to the boil and drop in the new potatoes to blanch for 6 minutes. Then add the salmon fillets, simmer until the fish is just cooked through, it should be creamy orange in the centre.

In another pan, blanch the vegetables, then take the salmon and potatoes out of the poaching liquid and allow to drain.

Toss the vegetables and potatoes in the olive oil and season.

To assemble the dish

Arrange the vegetables and potatoes on the plate with a wedge of lemon. Place the salmon on top and finish with herb emulsion.

CORN FED CHICKEN KIEV FILLED WITH WILD GARLIC & ORANGE BUTTER, BEETROOT & FETA SALAD

Serves 4

4 corn fed chicken supremes

125g butter, softened

1 orange, zested and segmented

20 young wild garlic leaves

4 cooked pickled beetroot

2 heads of baby gem

100g feta cheese, diced

16 sun blushed tomatoes

12 blanched sugar snap peas

Balsamic vinaigrette (page 229)

To make the garlic butter

Blanch the wild garlic in boiling water then refresh in ice cold water.

Drain, then squeeze out as much water as possible. Finely chop and mix with the butter and orange zest.

To stuff the chicken supreme

First, trim up the knuckle on the supreme with a boning knife, then make an insertion into the fat end of the breast. Run the knife through the centre being careful not to cut any holes.

Place the wild garlic butter in a piping bag and fill the pocket with the butter.

Refrigerate for half an hour so the butter firms up before crumbing.

For the crumb

6 tbsps fresh bread crumbs

6 tbsps polenta

4 tbsps grated parmesan

To crumb the kiev

4 tbsps flour

1 egg, beaten with 2 tbsps milk

1 crumb recipe

Dredge the chicken breast in flour, then beaten egg, and finally the bread crumb mixture. Coat completely, shaking off the excess.

To cook the kiev

Preheat the oven to 190ºC.

Heat some vegetable oil in an oven proof frying pan and fry the supremes until lightly browned. Transfer to the oven and bake for 18-20 minutes or until golden brown and completely cooked through.

To make the salad

First, cut off the bottom of the lettuce and break it up with your hands. Then quarter the beetroot, slice the sugar snap peas and mix in a bowl with the feta, orange segments and sun blushed tomatoes. Dress with vinaigrette.

To plate the dish

Place the salad at one side of the plate and the chicken on the other.

Serve with homemade chips.

BREAST OF FARMHOUSE CHICKEN FILLED WITH HOME CURED BACON & LEEK MOUSSE WITH TRUFFLED POTATO GRATIN

Serves 4

4 free range chicken
supremes

8 pancetta bacon rashers,
thinly sliced

4 slices of home cured bacon or
shop bought dry cured bacon

1 small leek

60ml double cream

1 tbsp of chopped chives

2 braised leeks (page 159)

Remove the inner chicken fillets
from the supremes, put the meat
into a food processor and blend
until minced. Add the double
cream and blend once more
until smooth, then season to taste
with salt and pepper.

Scrape any mince from the sides,
remove the chicken mousse from
the processor and place in a bowl
and refrigerate for 30-40 minutes.

Next finely dice the leek and
wash. Blanch in a pan of boiling
water for 2 minutes, then refresh
in cold iced water and drain.
Place to one side.

Finely dice the home cured bacon,
grill it and strain off any excess
grease and fat, then chill for 20
minutes.

Mix the leek, cooked home cured
bacon and snipped chives with the
chicken mousse and season. Once
the mixture is folded together
place inside a piping bag with a
round nozzle.

**To stuff the chicken supremes
with mousse**

Take each chicken supreme and
slice a pocket in the end using a
sharp knife and hollow it out into
the centre of the breast meat.

Next pipe the chicken mousse
into the pocket completely filling
it up so that the chicken breast
remains in its shape and is plump.

Place a piece of cling film on a
chopping board then add 2 slices
of pancetta bacon. Next, place the
chicken breast on top and roll it
over to create a chicken breast
shape with the pancetta bacon
wrapped around.

Make sure the cling film is tightly
wrapped around the breast, then
tie a knot in each end to secure it.

Place the chicken supremes on
a steamer tray and cook them
in a steamer oven, steaming for
approx 8-10 minutes until the core
of the supreme reaches 63ºC and
the chicken breasts are firm and
cooked. Remove from the oven
and the tray.

Chill them in the fridge for 2 hours
until they are completely cold and
chilled to 3ºC. Use a food probe
to check the temperature.

Potato gratin

15g butter

2 cloves of garlic, crushed

1kg potatoes, peeled and thinly
sliced (waxy ones are best)

1 large white onion, peeled and
thinly sliced

170g gruyere cheese, grated

150ml double cream

1 small white truffle, sliced

Salt and pepper

Grease an oven proof casserole
dish with soft butter and rub all
over with garlic.

First make a layer of sliced
potatoes, then onions, cheese
and truffle. Then season and add
a little cream. Continue, until the
final layer is potato.

Top with a little more grated
cheese then cover with foil and
place the dish in a pre heated
oven at 190ºC for 1 1/2 hours
until the potatoes are tender.
Remove the foil for the last 5
minutes so that the cheese turns
golden brown.

To cook chicken breasts

1 pinch of sea salt

1 pinch of black pepper

2 tbsps olive oil

2 knobs of butter

Take the chicken breasts from the
fridge, remove the cling film and
season. Place the olive oil and a
knob of butter into a frying pan
and heat.

When hot, place the chicken
breasts into the pan and quickly
fry on all sides until they are
golden brown. Then place in the
oven and cook for 8-10 minutes
or until they are hot and ready to
serve. Use a food probe to check
the temperature has reached
63ºC.

Cut the potato gratin into rounds,
then slice the chicken supremes
into 3 rounds and serve with
braised leeks and red wine sauce.

NORTHUMBRIAN HONEY & CLOVE BAKED HAM HOCK WITH YUKON GOLD MASH & PARSLEY CREAM SAUCE

Serves 4

4 ham hocks

1ltr white chicken stock

1 bay leaf

2 celery sticks, peeled, washed and cut into 3cm x 3cm cubes

1 onion, peeled and chopped

4 tbsps tomato purée

6 tbsps olive oil

4 tbsps clear honey

20 cloves

4 tbsps brown sugar

In a large heavy bottom pan, heat the olive oil and gently fry the carrot, celery and onion until soft and tender on a low heat.

Stir in the tomato purée, add the chicken stock and bay leaf and gently bring to the boil.

Add the ham hocks and simmer for around 3 hours or until the ham hocks are tender.

Once cooked, remove the hocks from the liquid and place on a tray to cool. Then remove the fat and outer meat from the hocks, leaving plump meat on the bone.

Individually wrap each hock tightly in cling film. Refrigerate for 6-8 hours.

To reheat the ham hocks, remove the cling film and place on a baking tray. Stud with the cloves, pour over the runny clear honey and sprinkle with demerera sugar.

Bake in an oven at 180ºC for approx 20 minutes or until crispy golden brown. Remember to baste after 10 minutes. Using a temperature probe make sure they reach 75ºC before serving.

Mash potato

500g Yukon gold potatoes

1/2 tbsp salt

150g cold butter, cut into cubes

100ml warm milk

Peel the potatoes and cut in to quarters. Rinse to remove any surface starch. Place in a medium size pan, cover with cold water and add a pinch of salt.

Gently bring to the boil and simmer for approx 30 minutes until tender.

Drain and briefly steam dry in the pan. Once the potatoes are dry and cool, use a potato masher to mash.

In a separate pan gently warm the milk and butter then pour over the mashed potato. Gently fold in and season with salt and white pepper to taste.

Parsley cream sauce

1 cup of dry white wine

2 large shallots, finely diced

1 cup of double cream

4 tbsps flat parsley, freshly chopped

Salt and pepper to taste

Combine the white wine and shallots in a small heavy saucepan and reduce by 2/3. This usually takes about 6 minutes.

Gradually add the double cream, bring back to boil then season and fold in the flat chopped parsley.

To serve

Warm the bowls and pour some parsley cream sauce to cover the base.

In the middle place a quenelle of hot Yukon gold mash. Sit the honey glazed ham hock on the mash and serve.

LAVENDER ROAST BREAST OF DUCKLING WITH TWO CELERIES, DRUNKEN FRUITS & NUTS

Serves 4

4 duckling breasts, trimmed of excess fat and sinew

1 head of celery

1/2 head of celeriac

1 quantity of drunken fruit

1 tbsp toasted pine nuts

4 sprigs of lavender

150ml brown chicken stock

Braised celery

500ml white chicken stock

100g butter

1 sprig of lemon thyme

Cut the celery in half, then into quarters and rinse in plenty of cold water.

Bring the chicken stock, butter and thyme to the boil, add the celery and braise. Cover with grease proof paper, simmering until tender. This will take about 15-20 minutes.

Celeriac purée

1/2 head of celeriac, diced to 1 cm dice

400ml milk

50g butter, cubed

Boil the celeriac in milk until very soft then strain the milk and reserve.

In a food processor, purée the celeriac, add a little of the milk and butter (a slice at a time) until you have a smooth purée.

Remove from the machine and pass through a fine sieve.

Season and keep warm until needed.

Drunken fruits

Serves 6

2 peaches, quartered and stoned

3 figs, quartered

4 ripe plums, quartered and stoned

10 pitted cherries

6 dried pitted dates

6 dried apricots

1 tbsp dried cranberries

1 cinnamon stick

1 vanilla pod, split

1 star anise

400ml red wine

100ml kirsch

200g brown sugar

In a medium size pan place the red wine, kirsch, brown sugar, star anise, vanilla pod and cinnamon stick. Bring to boil then drop in all the fruits and remove from the heat.

Leave at room temperature to cool.

These fruits can be made in advance and stored in an air tight container.

To cook the duckling breast

Pre heat the oven to 190ºC.

Place the duckling breast flesh side down on a chopping board, season with salt and pepper and a little lavender. Turn the breast over and season the skin with salt.

Next heat a frying pan until hot and add a film of vegetable oil.

Place the duckling breast skin side down and cook for 2 minutes or until crisp. Turn the breast over and place in the oven for 7-8 minutes at 190ºC.

Remove from the oven and allow to rest for 5 minutes before carving.

To assemble the dish

Warm the fruits, place in a glass and top with a few toasted nuts.

Using a dessert spoon place a dollop of the purée on the plate and using the back of the spoon stripe it across the plate.

Place the braised celery next to the purée then cut the duckling into 3 pieces and place around the celery.

Garnish with apple purée and serve with a gravy boat of the brown chicken stock.

CORNED BEEF

2.5kg rump of beef, diced

3ltr cold water

90g preserving salt

90g sea salt

1 level tbsp sel-rose

3 leaves of gelatine

1 sun blushed tomato, finely chopped

1 carrot, peeled and finely chopped

2 sticks of celery, peeled and finely chopped

1/4 whole nutmeg, grated

Black pepper, freshly ground

1/2 cup of parsley and chives, chopped

Use a non-reactive bowl, either glass or stainless steel.

To make the brine, mix the water and salts together until dissolved, then add the beef and mix well until all sides are covered so that the brine can penetrate the beef. Place a plate on top of the meat so that it is completely submerged in the brine and refrigerate.

After one day, stir the meat using a wooden spoon then return to the fridge for another day. After 2 days remove the beef from the brine and rinse thoroughly in cold water.

Add the beef to a large pan, cover with cold water, add the gelatine and bring to the boil. Once boiling, skim off any impurities that rise to the surface. Boil the beef for 3 hours, topping up the water when necessary.

Once the meat is breaking up, drain the liquid into another pan and reduce to 3/4 pint. Whilst the liquid is reducing, break up the beef using the back of a fork.

In a large bowl mix the beef, vegetables and chopped herbs. Add the beef stock, grated nutmeg and 20 turns of black pepper.

You will need 2 strong plastic containers 25cm by 20cm that will fit inside of each other.

Fill the first container full of the beef mixture and use the second container to press the beef. Place a 10kg weight on top and refrigerate overnight.

Once pressed, turn out onto a chopping board and cut to your desired size. This corned beef can be served hot or cold and will keep for 10 days or longer if vacuum packed.

RARE BREED PORK SAUSAGES WITH MUSTARD MASH & DEVILLED GRAVY

Serves 6

Mustard mash

1kg Lincolnshire potatoes, peeled and cut into quarters

100ml milk

50ml double cream

100g English mustard

1 pinch of sea salt

1 pinch of ground white pepper

Place the potatoes in a pan, cover with cold water and a lid. Bring to the boil and cook until tender (approx 15-20 minutes). Drain using a colander and leave to steam for a few minutes until dry and fluffy.

Rice the potatoes into a bowl, once smooth beat in the milk, cream, mustard and a good pinch of salt. Keep warm until needed.

Sausages

18 quality rare breed Chopwell pork sausages (locally sourced)

2 tbsps olive oil

2 knobs of butter

In a frying pan heat the olive oil and butter until hot. Quickly brown the sausages on all sides turning continuously until they are fully cooked and crisp golden brown, for approx 8-10 minutes. Remove from the frying pan and keep hot.

Devilled gravy

300ml good veal stock (reduced)

1 red onion, peeled and finely sliced

4 sprigs of thyme

1 red chilli, deseeded and finely diced

1 pinch of sea salt

Once you have removed the sausages from the frying pan, add the onion and gently fry until they are sticky and dark brown in colour. Next soften the diced chilli and add the sprigs of thyme.

Finally add the reduced veal stock, bring to the boil and gently simmer for a couple of minutes. Season with sea salt and serve.

To Assemble

Place a quenelle of mash in each of the six warm bowls, then add 3 sausages to each and finally pour over the devilled gravy.

BEAMISH RUMP STEAK BURGER WITH SWEET POTATO BUN

Serves 6

1kg rump steak, well trimmed

150g bone marrow

1 tbsp unsalted butter

1 small onion, peeled and finely chopped

3 tsps fresh oregano leaves

Sunflower Oil For Frying

To Garnish

6 beef tomato slices

6 red onion rings

6 gherkins, sliced

6 parmesan cheese slices

6 sweet potato buns

Pre heat the oven to 230ºC.

Remove all of the sinew and fat from the meat, then chop with a knife until it has a fine mince texture. Place in a large mixing bowl and grate in the bone marrow before mixing.

Heat the butter in a pan and sweat off the onions and oregano leaves without colouring until the onions are softened.

Allow the onions to cool then add the mince. Season well and gently mix together using your hands. Divide the mixture into six, then gently shape into 2.5cm thick rounds. Be careful not to pack them together too tightly.

Heat the oil in an ovenproof frying pan and sear the burgers on both sides before transferring to the oven. Cook for about 5 minutes for a medium rare burger.

INGRAM VALLEY LAMB WITH WHITE PEACH, CRUSHED POTATOES, PEAS & MINT

Serves 8

Confit of lamb shoulder

1 small lamb shoulder, boned out
(a local butcher will do this for you)

1 white onion, peeled and roughly
chopped

1 carrot, peeled and roughly
chopped

1/2 leek, washed and roughly
chopped

1/2 bulb garlic

2 sprigs of thyme

1/2 whole orange

Cold water, enough to cover
the lamb

1ltr white chicken stock

1 confit salt mix

150ml vegetable oil

In a deep roasting tray lay the
lamb shoulder skin side down and
sprinkle with confit salt mix. Cover
with cling film and store in the
fridge overnight.

To cook

Remove lamb shoulder from the
tray, and under cold running water
wash off the salt mix.

Then place in a large bowl and
continue to let cold water run over
the lamb for at least 20 minutes.

Remove the lamb and pat dry with
a clean tea towel or kitchen roll.

Place all of the vegetables in a
deep roasting tray and add the
lamb shoulder, skin side down on
top of these. Cover the lamb with
enough white chicken stock and
water and vegetable oil (which
should be half and half in quantity).

Cover the tray with foil and cook
in a slow oven for about 3 1/2
hours, until the meat is tender.
Once tender remove from the
oven and keep hot.

On a large work surface or kitchen
table, layer a roll of cling film and
smooth down to remove any air.
Repeat this 2 more times until
you have 3 layers.

Place the lamb in 1 piece onto a
clean tray using two fish slices or
slotted spoons. Remove all traces
of fat, skin and sinew, so that you
are left with pure meat. Whilst still
hot, lay the meat onto the cling film
to form a thin layer.

When all of the meat is stacked
up, gently lift the layer of cling film
close to the edge of the bench
and tightly roll into a thin sausage.

Once completely rolled and
covered in cling film, massage
the hot lamb with your hands so
that it gels together and there are
no gaps in the meat. Once this is
complete give the ends of the cling
film another gentle roll to shape
further. Then tie both ends very
tightly with string and prick all over
with a cocktail stick (you just need
tiny little pin pricks).

Then place on a tea cloth and with
both hands massage very gently to
remove any liquid. This will help to
compact the meat. Put one more
layer of cling film onto the work
bench, place the lamb confit onto
this, and roll again until completely
smooth and well compacted.

Refrigerate for 24 hours to
completely set.

For the spice mix

1/4 cup of smoked paprika

2 tbsps ground fennel seeds

2 tbsps ground cumin

1 tbsp ground coriander seeds

2 tbsps salt

1 tsp cinnamon powder

1 tsp cayenne pepper

1 tsp cracked pepper

Combine all of the ingredients in a bowl and stir. Then sieve, stir again and store in an air tight container.

To make the merguze sausages

500g minced lamb

120g finely chopped lardo or fat

3 cloves of garlic, crushed

2 tbsp coriander, freshly chopped

3 tsp harissa paste

2 tbsps merguze spice mix

Combine all of the ingredients in a bowl, knead the mixture well, shape as desired or grind in a meat grinder and feed into sausage skins, which can be purchased from any good butcher.

Crushed potatoes with pea and mint

Pumace olive oil and salt and ground pepper

500g Charlotte potatoes

20g fresh or frozen peas, blanched

1 small tin of Batchelors mushy peas

1 tbsp fresh mint, chopped

1/4 bag of spinach, washed and prepared

Cut the potatoes in half and cook in salted boiling water until tender.

Drain and leave to cool slightly.

Roughly crush the potatoes with a fork, add salt and pepper to taste and enough olive oil to bind together (a bit like adding butter to mash potatoes).

When the potatoes are cool mix in the rest of the ingredients and heat through in microwave when needed.

1 confit of lamb, rolled, sliced into 8 pieces

1 loin lamb, all sinew trimmed off, cut into 2 inch pieces

8 merguze sausages

4 poached white peaches, halved

300ml red wine sauce (page 221)

Pre heat the oven to 180ºC.

Season the lamb loin with salt and pepper on both sides. Heat a filament of oil in a non-stick frying pan and fry the lamb for 1 minute on each side then transfer to an oven tray.

Next fry the sausages for 30 seconds on each side, followed by the lamb shoulder. Place all of the meat in the oven for 6 minutes.

Remove from the oven and allow to rest for 4 minutes on a warm plate.

To plate the dish, heat the crushed potatoes and peas in the microwave, lay out the plates and pack the potatoes into a round non stick mould.

Slice your lamb loin into 6 pieces and place next to the potato. Place the lamb shoulder next to the loin, followed by the peach and top with the sausage. Pour over the red wine sauce.

BEAMISH VENISON & APRICOT CASSEROLE WITH A SAVOURY SAGE SCONE

Serves 4

For the casserole

100g flat parsley, chopped

600g venison haunch, seasoned

1 carrot, peeled and cut into
2 cm dice

1/2 celeriac, peeled and cut
into 2 cm dice

50g butter

6 tbsps olive oil

1 onion, finely diced

4 Charlotte potatoes, peeled

1 sprig of thyme

1 bay leaf

1 vanilla pod, split

4 star anise

1/2 cup of semi dried apricots

75cl Madeira/port

80ml brown chicken stock
(page 215)

Salt and pepper to season

1 cinnamon stick

1 tsp mixed spice

In a large thick casserole pan heat
the oil and butter until it starts to
smoke and foam. Quickly seal the
venison until it is golden brown in
colour.

Add the diced onion, Charlotte
potatoes, carrot and celeriac and
cook until equally coloured.

Turn the heat up and add the
Madeira and quickly reduce to
1/3 in the pan.

Then add the spice, star anise,
cinnamon stick, split vanilla pod
and gently cover with hot chicken
stock.

Cover with a lid and gently cook
for approx 1 1/2 hours or until the
meat is tender.

Add the apricots to the casserole
20 minutes before the end of the
cooking time to gently soften.

Once the casserole is ready to
serve, fold in the chopped flat
parsley then divide between
shallow serving bowls. Serve
with warm savoury sage scones.

For the savoury sage scones

125g self raising flour

1 tsp baking powder

1 pinch of maldon sea salt

20g unsalted butter, softened and
diced

1 sprig of fresh sage, chopped

1 large free range egg

50ml ice cold milk

Sift the flour, baking powder
and salt into a large bowl.
Then add butter and gently rub
together using the tips of your
fingers until the mixture is like
fine breadcrumbs. Next add the
chopped sage.

Make a well in the centre of
the bowl, in another bowl
whisk together the milk and egg,
then pour the mixture into the
centre of the well. Quickly mix
together, until you have a soft,
but not too sticky dough. Tip
the dough on to a lightly floured
surface and roll out with a rolling
pin.

Using a deep 8cm cutter, press
out as many rounds as you can.
Place the rounds on a baking tray
and brush the tops with milk.

Bake in a pre heated oven at
180ºC for about 20-25 minutes,
until they are golden brown and
have risen. The scones should be
'springy' when ready.

Remove and place on a wire rack
to cool.

Serve while still warm.

STEAK, KIDNEY & BROWN ALE PUDDING WITH BASHED CARROT & SWEDE

Serves 8

675g chuck steak, trimmed and cut into 2.5 cm cubes

350g ox kidney, trimmed and cut into small cubes

1 onion, peeled and finely diced

1 bottle of Newcastle Brown Ale

25g beef dripping

25g plain flour

400ml beef stock

salt and fresh ground black pepper

1 small bunch of flat leaf parsley, chopped

200g field mushrooms (optional)

1 quantity of bashed carrot and swede (see page 159)

Pre heat the oven to 180ºC.

Heat the dripping in a casserole dish, then season the beef and kidney and quickly colour on all sides until golden brown.

Add the onion and cook for a further 2 minutes, sprinkle with plain flour and mix in the beef stock and brown ale.

Place the lid on the casserole dish and cook in the oven for 2 hours.

Remove the casserole from the oven, allow to cool then taste and season. Fold in the finely chopped parsley and serve in large bowls.

Suet Pastry

560g self raising flour

1/2 tsp baking powder

1 pinch of salt

280g beef suet, chopped

4-6 tbsps iced water

110g unsalted butter

To make the pastry

Mix the flour, baking powder and salt in a bowl. Then rub in the suet and enough iced water to bind into a soft pliable dough. Leave to rest for 20 minutes.

To assemble suet pudding dariole

Line a dariole with cling film so that it covers the top of the mould.

On a lightly floured bench, roll out the pastry using a rolling pin. Then cut out a circle of pastry twice the size of the circumference of the dariole. Line the mould with pastry so that it overlaps the mould with at least 4cms hanging over the edge.

Fill the dariole to the top with cold steak and kidney stew. Fold over the overlapping pastry so that the pudding is completely sealed. Follow this by folding over the cling film and twisting at the top.

Cook for 40 minutes in a steam oven, then remove and leave to cool for a few minutes.

Serve immediately with bashed carrot and swede on top of some extra steak and kidney mix in a deep bowl.

VEGETABLES

SEMI DRIED PLUM TOMATOES

Serves 4

8 large vine ripened plum tomatoes

2 garlic cloves

1 tsp thyme, chopped

1 tsp oregano, chopped

Olive oil

Pre heat the oven to 100ºC.

Cut each tomato in half lengthways and cut the garlic into slivers, pushing them into the cut sides of the tomatoes. Sprinkle over the herbs and season with Maldon sea salt and pepper, drizzle generously with olive oil and place in the oven for 2 to 2 1/2 hours.

BUTTER BRAISED YOUNG LEEKS

4 young firm leeks

100g unsalted butter

300ml vegetable stock

2 sprigs of lemon thyme

1 pinch of sea salt

Slice the leeks in to 1 cm rounds and rinse in cold water.

In a small saucepan, bring the vegetable stock, butter, thyme and salt to the boil. Add the leeks then bring back to the boil and reduce the heat before covering with silicon paper.

Simmer for 10 minutes or until soft.

Be careful not to overcook, the leeks should be bright green but still tender.

CRUSHED CHARLOTTE POTATOES WITH PEAS & MINT

Olive oil and salt and ground pepper

500g Charlotte potatoes

20g fresh or frozen peas, blanched

1 small tin of mushy peas

1 tbsp fresh mint, chopped

40g picked spinach, washed

Cut the potatoes in half and cook in boiling salted water until tender. Drain and leave to cool slightly.

Roughly crush the potatoes with a fork, add salt and pepper to taste and enough olive oil to bind together (a bit like adding butter to mash potatoes).

When the potatoes are cooling down mix in the other ingredients.

BASHED CARROT & SWEDE

1 medium swede

2 medium carrots

30g butter

1 handful of fresh flat leaf parsley, finely chopped

Seasoning

Peel and dice the swede and carrot into 4cm chunks and place in a large saucepan, cover with water and bring to the boil.

Simmer for 1 hour or until soft.

Drain and bash together with the butter using a fork. Season with black pepper and salt and finish with finely chopped parsley.

VEGETABLE HOT POT

1 small orange fleshed sweet potato, peeled

1 small swede, peeled

1 small parsnip, peeled

1 small thick carrot, peeled

1 small celeriac, peeled

1 small baking potato, washed or 4 small mid potatoes

2 sprigs of thyme, picked and finely chopped

2 cloves of garlic, peeled and crushed

Salt and freshly ground black pepper

1 stem of butternut squash, unpeeled

1 medium white onion, peeled and thinly sliced

1 small red onion, peeled and thinly sliced

Hot vegetable stock

20g of butter

Seasoning

Pre heat the oven to 190ºC.

Cut all of the vegetables using a mandolin into wafer thin slices.

Place all of the sliced vegetables, except for the butternut squash into a large mixing bowl. Add the garlic and thyme and season well with salt and pepper.

Mix well with hands and evenly spread into a deep square casserole dish or roasting tray.

Place the butternut squash discs in neat rows over the vegetables until completely covered.

Fill half the dish with hot stock, add a few knobs of butter and cover tightly with foil and bake in a slow to medium oven until the vegetables are soft but not mushy.

After 1 hour remove the foil to allow the top to crisp up.

LENTIL
& ONION
DAHL

225ml measure red lentils

1/2 tsp ground tumeric

2 tbsps olive oil

1/2 tsp whole cumin

2 small dried chillies

1/2 small onion, diced

1 clove of garlic, crushed

Wash the lentils well in a large bowl of water, then drain and tip into a large pan.

Pour in 1.6 pints of water then bring to the boil, removing any scum that rises to the surface.

Stir in the tumeric, reduce the heat to low and partially cover with a lid slightly ajar.

Cook for 40 minutes stirring occasionally.

Heat the oil and add the cumin and chillies. As soon as the chillies crisp and darken, add the onions and cook until well browned.

Finally, add the garlic, cooking until golden.

Pour the mixture into the dahl and put a lid on it for about half an hour before serving.

MEDITERRANEAN FLAVOURS

2 red onions, peeled and quartered

1/2 butternut squash, cut into 2 cm dice

1 red pepper, deseeded, cut into 8 thick slices

1 yellow pepper, deseeded, cut into 8 thick slices

1 green pepper, deseeded, cut into 8 thick slices

1 small aubergine, cut into 1cm slices, dipped in the lemon juice

2 small courgettes, sliced into 1 cm rounds on an angle

1 bunch of asparagus

1 cup of marinated pitted olives

2 buffalo mozzarella balls, cut into 8 pieces

1/2 cup of sun-blushed tomatoes

8 marinated artichokes

75ml olive oil

3 tbsps red wine vinegar

1/2 lemon, juiced

Seasoning

Pre heat the oven to 180ºC.

Place the onions in a roasting tray, drizzle with olive oil, red wine vinegar and season with salt. Cook in the oven for 5 minutes until they start to brown, then cover with tinfoil and bake for 15 minutes or until tender.

Next, roast the squash, drizzle with a little olive oil and season. Cook for 15 minutes, or until tender, testing with a small knife. If the knife goes through with ease the squash is cooked.

Next heat a chargrill pan on a high heat and chargrill the rest of your vegetables in batches.

Blanch the asparagus in salted boiling water for 1 minute. Drain and mix all your vegetables, olives and sun blushed tomatoes together and place in the oven for 2 minutes to heat.

Remove from the oven and mix in your mozzarella, season and serve with a pesto of your choice.

ROASTED ROOTS

Serves 6 people

6 banana shallots, peeled

1 parsnip, peeled and cut into 1 cm dice

1 small celeriac, cut into 1 cm dice

2 sticks of celery, washed and cut into 5cm

1/2 butternut squash, deseeded and cut into 1cm

6 cloves of garlic, whole, skin left on

350g chantenay carrots, peeled and eyed

75ml olive oil

Sea salt and cracked black pepper

Pre heat the oven to 190ºC.

In a large roasting tray mix up all of the vegetables with olive oil, thyme, sea salt and ground black pepper.

Cover the tray with tin foil and slowly roast in the hot oven for 50-60 minutes, until they are soft, golden and crispy.

Remove the tray from the oven and discard the tin foil. Shake the tray around so that all of the vegetables are nicely coated in the olive oil.

Remove the garlic and serve.

YUKON GOLD MASH

Serves 6

1kg Yukon gold potatoes

100ml double cream

74g unsalted butter

1 pinch of grated nutmeg

Salt and pepper

Peel the potatoes and cut into quarters, place in a deep pot and add 1 tbsp of salt.

Cover with cold water and bring to the boil.

Turn the heat down to simmer. Test with a knife, when cooked drain into a pan.

In another pan, bring the butter to the boil and add the cream.

Rice the potatoes and add to the cream and butter mixture.

Season to taste.

DESSERTS

GINGER STICKY TOFFEE PUDDING, BUTTERSCOTCH SAUCE & VANILLA ICE CREAM

Serves 6-8

170g dates

170g caster sugar

170g self raising flour

60g butter

3 large free range eggs

1/2 vanilla pod, seeded

1 ball stem ginger, finely chopped

1 tsp bicarbonate soda

1/2 pint of water

Place the dates in a small pan, pour over 1/2 pint of cold water and bring to the boil. Once boiled remove from the heat and add the bicarbonate soda and stem ginger.

Cream the butter, sugar and vanilla, and add the eggs 1 at a time. Fold in the flour and finally add the date mixture with the liquid.

Pour into a cake tin and bake at 180ºC for 30-40 minutes.

Butterscotch Sauce

75g unsalted butter

75g demerara

75g golden syrup

125ml double cream

Place the butter, sugar and golden syrup in a medium sized saucepan.

Slowly bring to the boil once all of the sugar has dissolved.

Turn up the heat and boil for 5-7 minutes stirring constantly until the sauce has a golden brown colour.

Remove from the heat and stir in double cream.

175

CHOCOLATE, RASPBERRY & HAZELNUT TART WITH RASPBERRY SORBET

Serves 20

For the biscuit base

10 digestive biscuits, crushed

1/2 cup of hazelnuts, coarsley crushed

60g melted butter

Mix the biscuits, hazelnuts and melted butter in a mixing bowl. Pack into a 10 inch diameter, 1.5 cm high tart ring.

For the filling

2 punnets of raspberries

1kg dark chocolate

720ml whipping cream

Place the raspberries in the tart ring and chill for 10 minutes.

Boil the whipping cream, then remove from the heat, whisk in the chocolate then gently pour into the tart ring and chill until set.

Once set, use a blow torch to loosen the ring. Using a hot knife cut a portion and serve with raspberry sorbet. Top the tart with some crushed hazelnuts.

To make the sorbet

Serves 4

2 punnets of raspberries

200g caster sugar

250ml water

1 lemon, juiced

Place the sugar, water and raspberries in a pan and bring to the boil, then simmer for 10 minutes.

Add the lemon juice, then remove from the heat and blend to a purée in a blender.

Pass through a fine sieve, then transfer the mix to an ice cream machine to churn or pour into a container and freeze. You will have to stir the mixture every now and again until set.

VANILLA PANNACOTTA WITH FRESH BERRY MINESTRONE, ALMOND CRUNCH AND PLUM FRITTERS

Serves 4

Pannacotta

400ml double cream

100ml full fat milk

1 vanilla pod, split

100g sugar

2 leaves of gelatin (soaked in cold water)

Berry minestrone

2 punnets of mixed berries

1 quantity of light stock syrup (page 220)

6 mint leaves, chopped

Almond crunch

220g caster sugar

100g flaked almonds

1 squeeze of lemon juice

Plum fritters

15 mirabelle plums, pitted

170g self raising flour

1/2 pint cider

For the pannacotta

Boil the milk, cream, sugar and vanilla then remove from the heat and whisk in the soaked gelatin leaves.

Pass through a sieve and pour into dariole moulds.

Refrigerate for 4 hours until set.

For the berry minestrone

Bring the stock syrup to the boil then remove from the heat and pour over the berries and mint before refrigerating.

For the almond crunch

To make the caramel, add the sugar to a thick bottom pan and gently heat until brown around the edges.

Once all of the sugar is golden in colour add the flaked almonds and lemon juice. Then stir lightly with a wooden spoon and pour out onto a baking mat to cool.

Once cool, mix to a powder in a food processor. When the mix is fine pre heat the oven to 160ºC.

On a baking mat spread the mixture evenly, approx 3 mm thick, then place in the oven for 5 minutes.

Remove from the oven then place another mat on top and roll with a rolling pin.

Once cool remove both mats and place the almond crunch on the baking tray, then return

to the oven for 30 seconds. This will soften the biscuit for cutting.

Trim off the edges and cut into triangles, then allow to cool.

For plum fritters

To make the batter add flour to a mixing bowl, pour over the cider and whisk until smooth.

Add the pitted plums then deep fry at 350ºC for 4 minutes until crisp.

Drain on a paper towel then roll the fritters in a mixture of sugar and cinnamon.

To serve

To turn out the pannacotta, dip the mould into boiling water for a second.

Turn the pannacotta upside down, covering the open end of the mould with your hands. In a downward motion shake the mould, to allow the pannacotta to fall out.

Place in the middle of a bowl, then spoon some berries and syrup around.

Then place 3 of the fritters around the bowl, then add the almond crunch into the pannacotta to serve.

SUGAR GLAZED RICE PUDDING WITH CHERRY COMPOTE & BLACK CHERRY SORBET

Serves 4

100g pudding rice

700ml milk

300ml double cream

1 piece of orange peel

1 vanilla pod, split

50g caster sugar

1kg cherries

400g sugar

500ml water

1/2 a lemon, juiced

For the rice pudding

In a saucepan warm the milk, cream, orange peel, vanilla pod and seeds.

Add the rice and sugar and continue to stir at regular intervals for 30 minutes until the rice is tender, not allowing the rice to stick to the pan.

Remove the orange peel and vanilla pod and set aside until needed.

For the cherry compote and sorbet

Place the cherries in a thick bottom pan with 200ml of water and juice of half a lemon, bring to the boil, add the sugar and reduce by half. Remove 4 tbsps of the cherry compote to cool slightly then purée the mix in a blender with 500ml of water and pass through a sieve. This mix is for the black cherry sorbet, once cold add to a sorbet maker and churn to manufacturers recommendations.

Warm up the rice pudding with a little milk and pour over the compote, filling up the ramekins. Dust the top with caster sugar and glaze with a blow torch until caramelised. Top with a ball of the black cherry sorbet to serve.

PASTRY

250g plain flour

170g butter

1 large beaten egg

1/2 tsp water

1 pinch of salt

Mix the flour and chopped butter in a food processor for 30 seconds.

The mixture will resemble bread crumbs.

Add the beaten egg and mix for 5 seconds more, then remove from the mixer.

Turn out on to a bench and bring together with hands to form a ball.

Wrap in cling film and refrigerate for 20 minutes before use.

SWEET PASTRY

250g plain flour

170g butter

60g icing sugar

1 large beaten egg

1 vanilla pod, seeds

Mix the flour, chopped butter, icing sugar and vanilla pod seeds in a food processor for 30 seconds.

Then follow the directions shown above.

ITALIAN PEACH BAKEWELL

Serves 12

1 quantity of sweet pastry
(page 185)

4 whole white poached
peaches, halved and stoned

50g orange marmalade

225g soft butter

225g caster sugar

225g ground almonds

112g polenta flour

1 tsp baking powder

3 eggs, beaten

1 lemon zest, finely grated

1 orange zest, finely grated

1 cartouche, filled with
baking beans

1 handful of flaked almonds

Pre heat the oven to 160ºC.

Line a 10" tart ring with rolled
out sweet pastry and blind bake
using a cartouche filled with
baking beans for 10 minutes,
then put aside to rest.

In a bowl beat the butter and
sugar until creamy and pale,
then stir in the ground almonds.

Next, fold in the beaten eggs
1 level tbsp at a time. Then
add polenta, grated zests and
baking powder.

Spoon the mix into the blind
baked pastry until full.

Place the peach halves into the
mixture, gently pushing down
one at a time.

Place the cake on a baking tray
and cook for 45-50 minutes, or
until set and a deep golden
brown.

Warm the orange marmalade
in a small pan then brush on
top of the cake, spreading
evenly using a pastry brush.
Dust with flaked almonds.

Leave to cool then slice and
serve with peach ice cream.

CLASSIC VANILLA ICE CREAM

Makes 1.5ltr

500ml whole milk

500ml double cream

180g caster sugar

12 large egg yolks

2 vanilla pods

To make the crème anglaise

Put the milk and cream in a saucepan.

Beat the sugar and egg yolks in a heatproof bowl. Split the vanilla pods and scrape out seeds and add to the sugar and eggs.

Then add the empty vanilla pods to the milk and cream and bring to the boil before gradually pouring onto the sugary mixture.

Strain the mix through a sieve and pour back into the pan and warm on low heat. Stir constantly with a wooden spoon until the custard thickens slightly, enough to thinly coat the back of the spoon.

Strain back through the sieve and cover with cling film, then refrigerate. Stir occasionally to ensure a skin does not form then churn in an ice cream machine.

To make pistachio ice cream
Add 6 tbsps of pistachio compound to the hot custard.

To make peach ice cream
Add 5 poached puréed peaches to the cold custard.

To make lemon curd ice cream
Add 300ml of lemon curd to the milk and cream. Use half the amount of egg yolks and sugar.

WITH COFFEE BEAN SAUCE & PISTACHIO ICE CREAM

Serves 10

275g bitter chocolate, chopped

225g unsalted butter

400g caster sugar

200g plain flour, sifted

5 eggs

100g pistachio nuts, chopped and blanched

250ml whole milk

5 tsps instant coffee

200g dark chocolate callets

50g caster sugar

In a pan gently warm up the milk and sugar. When hot pour into a bowl over the coffee granules and chocolate callets. Whisk until smooth, shiny and silky.

In a bowl set over a saucepan of simmering water, heat the chocolate and butter, then whisk in the sugar and beat in the eggs.

Fold in the flour, then the blanched chopped pistachio nuts.

Line the 7cm diameter by 2cm deep baking rings with butter.

Pour in the mix and cook in a pre heated oven at 150ºC until the brownies are set on the outside and soft in the middle.

In the middle of a plate, place a warm brownie with a little coffee bean sauce.

Finish with a big scoop of homemade pistachio ice cream and a few pistachio nuts.

CLASSIC CRÈME CARAMEL WITH BRANDY BASKET OF ORANGE SORBET

Classic crème caramel

250g caster sugar

4 tbsps liquid glucose

300ml double cream

75ml full fat milk

2 leaves of gelatine, soaked in water

25ml water

First, to make the caramel, put 100g of sugar into a pan, add the glucose and 25ml of water.

Place over a low heat and stir occasionally until the liquid no longer feels gritty.

Fill a basin with iced water.

When the liquid is a golden caramel colour, remove from the heat and place the pan into the iced water basin. This will allow the liquid to cool without continuing to cook.

When cool, spoon approx 2 tbsps into each dariole mould and leave to set.

Add the cream and milk to a pan and slowly bring to the boil, then reduce a little for 5 minutes.

Remove from the heat and fold in the remaining 150g caster sugar, then add the squeezed gelatine and stir quickly.

Once the cream is cool, slowly pour onto the caramel in the dariole moulds, filling them to the top.

Refrigerate until set for 4-6 hours.

To serve, dip the dariole moulds in hot water for a few seconds, then pull the set cream away from the sides. Invert and shake out on to individual dessert plates.

Brandy snap basket

65g unsalted butter, softened

125g caster sugar

65g golden syrup

65g plain flour, sifted

1 tsp oil

Mix the butter, sugar, golden syrup and flour in an electric mixer with paddle beater for approx 5 minutes until smooth.

Refrigerate for 24 hours.

Heat the oven to 180ºC.

Place a non stick baking mat on a baking tray. Roll the brandy snap mix into little balls approx 1cm, then place on the tray and gently push down until they are flat.

Cook for about 8 minutes, until they turn a golden brown colour.

Leave to cool on the baking mat for a few seconds, then place a dariole mould upside down and gently oil the mould.

Once cool, remove the biscuit from the tray and place over the dariole using a palette knife.

Gently push the sides of the biscuit outwards to create a basket shape, then leave to set.

Once the biscuit is brittle, gently remove the crisp brandy snap basket from the dariole mould and turn the right way up.

To make the orange sorbet

10 oranges, juiced and zested

200g golden caster sugar

2 tbsps orange flower water

1 large egg white

Put the zest, juice, sugar and 200ml water in a pan and heat gently to dissolve the sugar. Bring to the boil and boil for 1 minute, then set aside to cool.

Stir the orange flower water into the cooled syrup, cover and refrigerate for 30 minutes.

Strain the orange syrup into a bowl. In another bowl whip the egg white until just frothy, then whisk into the orange mixture.

For best results, freeze using an ice cream machine. Otherwise, pour into a shallow freezer proof container and freeze until almost frozen, then mash well with a fork and freeze until solid.

Transfer the sorbet to the fridge 30 minutes before serving.

To plate the dish

Place a brandy basket next to the crème caramel, then scoop a ball of the orange sorbet into the basket and serve with a few orange segments.

STRAWBERRY & MASCARPONE SPONGE WITH MERINGUE & ROSEWATER SYRUP

Serves 8

225g caster sugar

80ml water

6 eggs, separated

60g plain flour

50g cornflour

1 tsp baking powder

Boil the sugar and water until it forms a soft ball. Use a sugar thermometer to monitor the temperature.

Using an electric whisk, whisk the egg whites into soft peaks, gradually pour the sugar syrup into the meringue.

Add the egg yolks 1 at a time and mix then fold in the dry ingredients.

Butter and flour 10 dariole moulds then fill 2/3 full and bake at 170°C for 10-15 minutes.

Rosewater syrup

250g caster sugar

250ml water

1 vanilla pod

1 orange zest

1 lime zest

1 lemon zest

2 red roses

Boil the sugar and water with the vanilla and zests until a soft ball is formed. At this stage, small pea size bubbles will start to form.

Remove from the heat and add the rose petals, reserving some for garnishing.

Leave the syrup to infuse until cold.

Marinated strawberries

2 punnets of strawberries

25ml water

25g caster sugar (water and sugar made into a 50 stock syrup)

25ml strawberry liqueur

Dice the strawberries and marinate in the syrup and liqueur.

Italian meringue

300ml caster sugar

1 heaped tbsp glucose syrup

80ml water

6 egg whites

Boil the sugar, glucose and water to 110°C then whisk the egg whites into soft peaks.

Gradually pour the sugar into the egg whites. Whisk using an electric whisk until thick, glossy and cool.

Pipe meringue fingers onto silicon paper or a drying mat, then bake at 60°C for 2 hours.

Strawberry crisps

2 punnets of strawberries

250ml water

250g caster sugar (water and sugar boiled into sugar syrup)

Thinly slice the strawberries and dip them into sugar syrup, then layer them close together on a drying mat.

Dry overnight in an oven at its lowest temperature then store in an airtight container until needed.

Mascarpone

500g softened mascarpone

To assemble the dish

Using a knife hollow out the sponge and fill with the marinated strawberries.

Using a palette knife, apply the mascarpone to the sponge and press on the meringue and dried rose petals.

Drizzle with the rosewater syrup to serve.

RASPBERRY & LIME LEAF BRULÉE WITH SHORTBREAD BISCUITS

Serves 4

125g caster sugar

3 egg yolks

1/2 pint double cream

1 punnet raspberries

8 lime leaves

In a saucepan warm the double cream and infuse the lime leaves. Then remove the lime leaves and leave to cool.

In a bowl whisk together the egg yolks and sugar until white and fluffy. Sieve the cream into the egg mix and whisk.

Place 5 raspberries in each of the 4 ramekins and pour in the crème brulée.

Place the ramekins into a roasting tray and fill the tray with water until it reaches half way up the sides of the ramekins.

Cook in a pre heated oven at 120ºC for 45 minutes, until they are just set in the middle.

Remove and leave to cool for 2 hours in the fridge.

To serve

Sprinkle the brulee with approx 2 tbsps caster sugar and glaze with a blow torch, turning the surface into a dark golden brown caramel.

Serve with 4 small shortbread biscuits on each plate and a few berries.

For the shortbread biscuits

110g unsalted butter

50g caster sugar

110g plain flour

50g rice flour

Beat the butter until soft, then add the sugar and beat until pale.

Sift the flour, then add the butter and lightly mix.

Place a 15cm flan ring on a baking tray, press the mixture into the ring and dust with some extra caster sugar.

Refrigerate for 30 minutes.

Pre heat the oven to 170ºC and bake for 40 minutes until a pale biscuit colour is achieved.

Allow to cool slightly before cutting into round biscuits.

BREAD

MY BREAD

5 loaves

1.5kg tipo 00 / strong flour

75g fresh yeast

45g lard / fat

35g salt

15g dough conditioner

30g semi skimmed milk powder

600ml tepid water

To make the dough, place the flour, yeast, conditioner, lard, salt and milk powder in a large bowl and make a well in the middle.

Pour in most of the tepid water. Use a wooden spoon or fingers to combine the ingredients into a workable, pliable dough.

Place the rolled dough onto a floured surface and knead for at least 10 minutes or until smooth and elastic. This can also be done in a mixer with a dough hook.

Place the dough in a clean oiled bowl, cover with cling film and leave to rise until doubled in size.

Pre heat the oven to 220ºC.

Knead the dough on a floured surface, pushing the air out. Mould into 400g shapes and place in an oiled loaf tin. Leave to prove again until doubled in size.

Slice the top with a knife and bake the bread for about 20-25 minutes, then reduce the oven temperature to 170ºC and continue to bake for another 15-20 minutes, or until the loaf sounds hollow when removed from the tin.

Leave the warm bread on a wire rack to cool.

To make olive and rosemary focaccia

Divide the dough in half and shape into rectangles, then place
in oiled tins. Leave to rise for 1 hour or until doubled in size.

Using your fingertips, make dimples all over the surface of the
dough, stud with olives and rosemary and drizzle with garlic oil.
Then sprinkle with sea salt and finally spray with water, bake at
200ºC for 25 minutes.

Once cooked remove from the oven and drizzle with olive oil.

To make sun-blushed tomato, tear and share bread

Roll out the dough on a floured work surface. Use a large cooks knife to cut the dough into strips and mix with sun blushed tomatoes (herbs optional). Then place on an oiled baking tray and prove in a warm place until doubled in size.

Drizzle with some of the oil from the sun blushed tomatoes and sprinkle with sea salt, then bake at 200ºC for 15 minutes or until golden.

SWEET POTATO BUN

750g tipo 00 flour

500g sweet potato purée

15g skimmed milk powder

7g dough conditioner

20g lard / butter

50g fresh yeast

400ml tepid water

To make the sweet potato purée, microwave the potatoes on a microwaveable plate, on high power for 10 minutes until soft.

Half the potato and scoop out the flesh with a tablespoon, discarding the skin. Use a potato ricer to rice the sweet potato, then leave to cool before using.

Mix the dry ingredients and sweet potato in a mixing machine using the dough hook, adding water in a constant stream.

Mix to a smooth dough adding a little more flour if the mix becomes too sticky.

Then knead the dough for 15 minutes and shape into buns.

Prove in a warm place until doubled in size.

Pre heat the oven to 180ºC.

Once doubled in size brush with a little milk and sprinkle with sea salt. Bake for 20-30 minutes until golden.

BLACK TREACLE BREAD

750g tipo 00 flour

750g granary flour

30g skimmed milk powder

15g dough conditioner

45g lard

75g fresh yeast

800ml tepid water

300g black treacle

Add the dry ingredients to a mixer.

Mix together the treacle and water, then pour steadily into the dry mixture. Knead using a dough hook to make a smooth dough.

This should take 15 minutes.

Shape the dough to 400g, mould and reset for 10 minutes.

Brush the top with olive oil, sprinkle with sea salt, prove, and then bake.

STOCKS AND SAUCES

VEGETABLE STOCK

Makes 1.5ltr

3 onions, peeled and coarsely chopped

1 washed leek, coarsely chopped

2 celery sticks, coarsely chopped

1 whole head of garlic, split in half

1 lemon, cut into wedges

1/4 tsp whole white peppercorns

1/2 bay leaf

4 whole star anise

2ltr cold water

1 sprig of: tarragon, basil, thyme, coriander and parsley

200ml dry white wine

Place the vegetables and the lemon wedges, peppercorn, bay leaf and star anise in a large saucepan. Add water and bring to boil, then simmer for 10 minutes.

Remove from the heat, add wine and fresh herbs making sure they are deeply submerged.

Leave to one side and cool.

When the stock is cool place into plastic containers and store in the refrigerator to infuse.

After 12 hours strain through a muslin lined colander.

The stock is now ready to use.

WHITE CHICKEN STOCK

2kg chicken wings or carcasses

4ltr cold water

3 celery sticks, coarsely chopped

2 leeks, coarsely chopped

2 large onions, peeled and quartered

2 large carrots, peeled and coarsely chopped

1/4 head of garlic, unpeeled

2 sprigs of thyme

parsley stalks

Rinse the chicken wings or bones in cold water to remove any blood, then drain and place in a large pan. Add water and bring to the boil, skimming with a ladle.

Add all of the ingredients and mix well. Bring to the boil and simmer gently for 4 hours. Then remove the bones and vegetables and strain through muslin cloth into a clean pan.

To add an Asian flavour to the white chicken stock

2 star anise

1 cinnamon stick

1 red chilli, split

1 bunch of coriander

1 piece of fresh ginger

2 garlic cloves, crushed

1 tsp brown sugar

1 splash of Chinese rice wine

BROWN CHICKEN STOCK

2kg chicken wings

4ltr cold water

3 celery sticks, coarsely chopped

2 leeks, coarsely chopped

2 large onions, quartered

2 large carrots, peeled and coarsely chopped

1/4 head of garlic, unpeeled

1 large sprig of thyme

4 large tbsps tomato purée

2 tbsps milk powder

Dust the chicken wings in the milk powder, then roast for 30 minutes at 200ºC until dark golden brown.

In a large thick bottom pan add a tbsp of vegetable oil and place on a medium heat, until just starting to smoke.

Then add the vegetables and stir continuously until they turn brown. Keep stirring for 5 minutes to ensure they do not burn, then add water, thyme and chicken wings or carcasses.

Cook for 4 hours on a low simmer, skimming all of the time.

Once cooked, remove the vegetables and bones then pass the stock through a fine muslin and colander.

COURT BOUILLON

Makes 2.25ltr

2 carrots, peeled and cut thin into 3mm rounds

1 white part of leek, cut thin into 3mm rounds

1 stick of celery, cut thin into 3mm rounds

1/2 bulb of fennel, cut thin into 3mm rounds

4 shallots, peeled and cut thin into 3mm rounds

1 small white onion, cut thin into 3mm rounds

2 garlic cloves, roughly crushed

2 tarragon stalks, 1 bay leaf, 2 parsley stalks

1 pinch of caraway seeds

6 black pepper corns

3 whole cloves

25g sea salt

250ml dry white wine

1 whole lemon, cut into three

2 tbsps white wine vinegar

Place all of the ingredients in a poaching pan.

Bring to the boil and leave to one side ready to poach the fish or chicken.

FISH STOCK

Makes 2ltr

1kg white fish bones (turbot or sole), rinsed in running cold water for 10 minutes

1 white onion, peeled and roughly chopped

1 stick of celery, roughly chopped

100ml dry white wine

2ltr water

6 parsley stalks

1 bay leaf

Sweat the vegetables over a low heat with white wine until soft. Then add the fish bones, stirring continuously for 2-3 minutes.

Next add the water, parsley stalks and bay leaf and bring to the boil and skim. Then simmer for 20 minutes, constantly skimming the stock.

Take off the heat and leave to stand for 10 minutes then strain through a muslin lined colander.

SHELL FISH STOCK

1ltr of fish stock

50g langoustines shells (raw ones are best)

50g lobster or crab shells

50g prawns, shell on

1/2 large carrot, peeled and finely chopped

2 cloves of garlic, crushed

1/2 bulb of fennel finely chopped

1/4 of a white onion, finely chopped

2 tsp tomato purée

1/2 tsp fennel seeds

1/2 glass of white wine

1/2 glass of brandy

In a thick bottom pan or tray place the crab shells, prawns (with shells) and langoustine shells and crush roughly with a rolling pin.

Then mix in a food processor until you get a thick boney mush.

Meanwhile in a thick bottom pan sweat the vegetables with the wine and reduce by half. Then add the seafood mix, fennel seeds and tomato purée and cook for 2 more minutes and flame with brandy.

Add the fish stock and cook for 30 minutes, then strain through a fine sieve.

VEAL STOCK

2kg veal or beef bones, chopped eg. pig trotters

2 large onions, coarsely chopped

2 large carrots, coarsely chopped

2 celery sticks, coarsely chopped

1/4 head of garlic

3 tbsps tomato purée

200g flat mushrooms

1 bunch of thyme

Pre heat the oven to 220ºC. Place the bones in a large roasting pan and roast until golden brown, turning every now and again. This should take just under an hour.

Meanwhile, place all vegetables in a large pan and cook until golden brown, then add the tomato purée and cook for 5 minutes, stirring so that it does not burn.

Add the water and bones and bring to boil, then skim off any scum.

Lower the heat and simmer very gently for 8 hours, skimming any fat off every so often.

Discard any bones and vegetables then drain through muslin into a clean pan. Reduce by half on a high heat, skimming all of the time.

Cool, then use as required.

LIGHT STOCK SYRUP

Makes about 1 1/2 pints

450g caster sugar

1 whole cinnamon stick

600ml water

1 star anise

1 orange peel

1 lemon peel

1 vanilla pod, split and seeded

Place all of the ingredients in a pan.

Dissolve the sugar in water by bringing to the boil slowly, sieving to ensure that all of the sugar dissolves.

Boil the syrup for 1 minute. Sieve, cool and store in a screw top jar in a cool place.

MUSTARD CREAM

1 shallot, finely diced

100ml white wine

500ml white chicken stock

500ml double cream

1 tbsp pommery mustard

Add the shallot and white wine to a saucepan and reduce by half. Then add chicken stock and reduce by half again.

Next add the double cream, then mustard and reduce to the correct consistency.

RED WINE JUS

500ml Shiraz red wine

1 carrot, thinly sliced

2 shallots, thinly sliced

1 stick of celery, thinly sliced

1 tbsp glucose syrup

2 sprigs of thyme

2 cloves of garlic

500ml veal stock

Add the vegetables and red wine to a saucepan and reduce by half.

Then add the veal stock and bring to the boil.

Strain into a clean pan and reduce to a syrup consistency.

DRESSINGS

TOMATO AND CHILLI JAM

500g ripe plum tomatoes

4 large red chillies

4 cloves of garlic, peeled

2 thumbs of ginger, peeled and chopped

30ml Thai fish sauce

300g palm sugar

100ml red wine vinegar

Blend half of the tomatoes, chilli, garlic, ginger and fish sauce.

Then put the purée, sugar and vinegar in a deep pot and bring to the boil, stirring constantly. When it reaches the boil, turn the heat down to a gentle simmer.

Dice the remaining tomatoes to 1/2 cm dice and add them to the pan.

Bring back to the boil and skim off any impurities, using a ladle.

Gently cook for 30-40 minutes, stirring every 5 minutes.

When the jam is ready, pour into warm glass jars and allow to cool at room temperature before storing in the fridge.

LEMON CURD

280g caster sugar

280g unsalted butter

100g egg yolk

4 lemons, zest and juices

Place the sugar, butter, lemon juice and zest in a bowl and stir over a pan of simmering water.

Using an electric whisk, beat until combined.

Then beat in the egg yolks and continue to cook for 15-20 minutes until the curd has thickened.

Once cooled, pour into sterilised jars and seal tightly.

This should keep for at least 2 weeks if refrigerated.

ORANGE AND GINGER MARMALADE

1kg of Seville oranges

2 lemons, juice

2.5kg granulated sugar

100g root ginger, peeled and grated

3ltr water

Squeeze the juice from all of the oranges. Trap the pips in a plastic container and put into a muslin bag with the membrane of the oranges and grated ginger.

Shred a proportion of the skin from the oranges and mince the rest or chop finely by hand.

Put the shred and minced peel into a bucket along with the juice from the lemons and oranges with the tied up muslin bag and cold water. Place in the fridge over night.

After soaking, put the contents of the bucket including the muslin bag into a preserving pan and bring to boil.

Simmer gently for about 2 hours then remove the bag and squeeze out the juice. After boiling you should have 1700ml of liquid.

Add the sugar to the pan, stirring to ensure it does not catch the bottom of the pan. When the sugar has dissolved, bring to a full boil, then boil at a relaxed heat to make sure the marmalade does not spill over.

Skim occasionally and boil until 105ºC is reached. Use a sugar thermometer to monitor this setting point. Ladle into sterilised jars whilst still warm.

MARINATED OLIVES

1kg mixed olives

500ml vegetable oil

250ml extra virgin olive oil

5 sprigs of rosemary

5 cloves of garlic, bashed

10 sun dried tomatoes

Sterilise five jars in boiling water then place in the oven at 180ºC for 10 minutes. Remove and allow to cool.

Fill each jar with olives and add a piece of rosemary, 1 clove of garlic and 2 pieces of sun dried tomato.

Warm the oil to 65ºC, then pour over the olives and vacuum seal with a lid whilst warm.

TERIYAKI MARINADE

1 cup of dark soy

1 cup of water

3/4 cup of sugar

1/4 cup of worcester sauce

3 tbsps distilled vinegar

1 tsp onion powder

2 tsps garlic powder

1 tbsp fresh ginger, grated

1 lemongrass stick, bashed

Combine all of the above ingredients.

This marinate is good for fish, chicken, beef or pork.

SUN BLUSHED TOMATO PESTO

1 cup of sun blushed tomatoes, roughly chopped

1 garlic clove, crushed

150ml olive oil

1/4 cup of toasted pine nuts

1/4 cup of parmesan, finely grated

10 basil leaves, chopped

1 tsp smoked paprika

Put the sun blushed tomatoes, garlic, nuts, paprika and olive oil into a food processor and purée to a coarse paste.

Place in a mixing bowl, add the parmesan and basil, then season.

BALSAMIC DRESSING

125ml balsamic vinegar

250ml olive oil

2 tbsps demerera sugar

2 tbsps balsamic syrup

1 pinch of salt

Combine all of the ingredients in a bowl and whisk until all of the sugar has dissolved.

CAESAR DRESSING

250ml mayonnaise

2 tbsps parmesan, grated

2 white anchovy fillets, finely chopped

1 clove of garlic

75mls olive oil

1/2 tsp pommery mustard

Seasoning

Mix all of the ingredients in a food processor until emulsified and smooth. Season to taste.

BLACK BEAN DRESSING

2 star anise

2 cups olive oil

1/2 cup dried black beans

2 tbsps sesame oil

1 tbsps nam pla, fish sauce

4 tbsps dark soy

1 stick lemongrass, bashed

1 lime leaf

1 clove garlic, crushed

1 tbsp fresh ginger, peeled and finely sliced

1 spring onion, finely sliced

1/2 red bell pepper, deseeded and finely sliced

1 small bunch of fresh coriander, finely chopped, with stalks removed

1 chilli, deseeded and finely chopped

Place the oils, fish sauce, lime leaf, star anise, lemongrass and the fresh coriander stalks in a saucepan. Gently and slowly increase the heat, then remove and leave to cool and infuse for 1 hour.

Pass through a fine sieve.

Place all of the other ingredients in a bowl and gently pour over the oil and mix.

Place in a fridge until ready to serve.

PISTACHIO PESTO

4 cups of rocket or basil, chopped

1 clove of garlic, crushed

150ml oil

1/4 cup blanched pistachio nuts

1/4 cup parmesan, finely grated

Seasoning

Put the herbs, garlic, pistachio nuts and olive oil in a food processor and purée to a coarse paste. Place in a mixing bowl and add the parmesan and seasoning. Add a little more olive oil to achieve the required consistency.

Season to taste.

ARTICHOKE PESTO

6 artichokes, marinated in sunflower oil

1 clove garlic

1/4 cup of blanched almonds

1/4 cup of parmesan, finely grated

150ml of olive oil

Salt to taste

Put the artichokes, garlic and almonds in a food processor and purée to a coarse paste, then pour in the oil. Place in a mixing bowl, then add the parmesan and seasoning.

Store in a jar and refrigerate.

ASIAN DRESSING

6 tbsps light soy sauce

6 tbsps mild vinegar

2 tbsps vegetable oil

4 tbsps sesame oil

8 tbsps sugar

1/2 tsp salt

2 limes, juiced

1 tsp toasted sesame seeds

1 red chilli, seeds removed and finely diced

1 handful of coriander leaves, chopped

Combine all of the above ingredients in a bowl and whisk.

Leave for 1 hour to infuse before use.

SOYA MILK AND LIME DRESSING

500ml soya milk

200ml lime juice

100g castor sugar

4 drops of red food colouring

Whisk together all of the ingredients and add a little more sugar if desired.

This dressing is good for hot chicken salads and also grilled prawn salads.

BLOODY MARY DRESSING

Makes 500ml

300ml good quality mayonnaise

200ml tomato ketchup

1 tbsp tabasco sauce

1 tbsp worchester sauce

50ml vodka

1 tbsp tomato purée

Combine all of the ingredients in a mixing bowl and whisk.

Store in an air tight jar for over 1 week.

SWEET MUSTARD DRESSING

1 tbsp cider vinegar

1 tbsp pommery mustard

3 tbsps rapeseed or olive oil

1 tbsp clear honey

Seasoning

In a bowl mix the cider vinegar, honey, pommery mustard and rapeseed oil. Whisk then season.

RASPBERRY & HAZELNUT DRESSING

1 punnet of fresh raspberries

50ml hazelnut oil

1 tsp honey

1/2 tsp Dijon mustard

50ml olive oil

60ml red wine vinegar

1 small clove of garlic

1 pinch of salt

Place the raspberries, garlic, red wine vinegar and mustard in a blender.

Add the salt and honey, then whilst blending drizzle in both of the oils.

Cover and store in the fridge then serve at room temperature.

This dressing is good with fish. You could add a splash of Tabasco sauce to spice it up.

BEAMISH PARK HOTEL EMPLOYEES

KITCHEN

CHRISTOPHER WALKER
MARTIN BLACK
ALAN RUSSELL
TERRY BATEY
DOROTHY BROTHERS
ANDREW WADE

HOUSEKEEPING

JULIE FRAZER
PEGGY WILSON
JOYCE IRWIN
CHRISTINE IRWIN
AMY IRWIN
JEANNIE SHIELD
SUSAN ANDERSON

BAR/RESTAURANT

JULIA DAVISON
PAUL WILLIS
QUINTINO VELHO
JEAN WOLF

BAR/RESTAURANT CASUAL/PART TIME

DAVID TAYLOR
KELLY CRITCHLOW
LAUREN MENNELL
ETHAN STEEL
ALEX DOUGHERTY
MATTHEW ROBERTS
CAROLINE GUY
ANNA MENNELL
JULIE WOLF

RECEPTION/SALES

SANDRA DEVLIN
WENCHE ROMSLO
JESS KEVAN
ROSIE ROACH
KAYLEIGH GREGORY
JOHN MILLER
MARTIN WILKINSON

MANAGEMENT

SUSAN LILLEY
PAUL DAVISON

SPECIAL THANKS AND GRATITUDE TO

CLIVE IMBER

MARTIN CHARLTON

MICHAEL POWNEY

DOROTHY HOPE

MARIAN & JOS LUMSDALE

INDEX

INDEX